Guide F

Help in surviving the stages of grief and bereavement after a loss

Rodger Murchison

Read The Spirit Books

an imprint of
David Crumm Media, LLC
Canton, Michigan

For more information and further discussion, visit
http://www.GuideForGrief.com

Cover art and design by
Rick Nease, www.RickNease.com
Illustrations by Sara Pollock Searle

Published By
Read The Spirit Books
an imprint of
David Crumm Media, LLC
42015 Ford Rd., Suite 234
Canton, Michigan, USA

For information about customized editions, bulk purchases
or permissions, contact David Crumm Media, LLC at info@
DavidCrummMedia.com

Contents

Dedication

THIS BOOK IS DEDICATED to the memory of my parents, Thomas and Florence Murchison. In their living, they taught me valuable lessons about life. And in their dying, they taught me valuable lessons about grief. This book will reflect much of what I learned from these faithful and dedicated parents.

Acknowledgments

TO ME, ALL OF life is a reaction to relationships. As you read this book, I would like you to know some of the relationships that have made this book possible.

The support and encouragement of so many family and friends have been invaluable. My wife, Margaret, has been so faithful and understanding throughout the process of writing this book. She began by proofreading my doctoral dissertation that became the foundation for the book. She has continued to be a support as she has read every draft of the book process.

I am also grateful to my children, Mitchell and Rebecca, who sacrificed time with their father as I committed an inordinate amount of energy to the dissertation and the book.

The faculty and administrators at Princeton Theological Seminary were most helpful during the formation of my thought that culminated in the dissertation topic, "Grief and Faith: A Study of Effect."

Regent's Park College at Oxford University in Oxford, England and The Bill Marshall Center for Ministry at Georgetown University in Georgetown, Kentucky provided valuable resources for research and an inspiring setting for preparation of the book manuscript.

Valparaiso Ministry Scholarship Program from Valparaiso University in Valparaiso, Indiana gave a generous grant to assist in funding the research for the book manuscript.

Anna Bannister, Eileen Martin and Frank Vaughn, all church members at First Baptist Church Augusta, GA, proofread the manuscript and all gave constructive suggestions for improvement.

Dede Maddox, Pastoral Associate at First Baptist Church Augusta, read very carefully the final drafts of the book and made many helpful comments.

The beautiful and creative artwork of Sara Pollock Searle adds a wonderful graphic dimension to this book. I appreciate Sara's artistic sensitivity as she used the medium of watercolor to interpret each chapter.

The book publishers, David Crumm and John Hile, have given me such good counsel during the process of developing this book. I am also very indebted to Celeste Dykas, the copy editor, who has read the manuscript, over and over, in an attempt to make sure every word in this book is correct. Celeste, I am grateful for your patience and your professionalism in your role as copy editor.

I cannot say enough about the support I received from the congregation of First Baptist Church Augusta, Georgia. The Continuing Education and Sabbatical Leave Programs the church so graciously provided, made much of this book possible. The church also gave me the opportunity to conduct a biannual Grief Ministry Workshop that ministered to those in grief and helped me explore many of my ideas concerning grief. Numerous church members encouraged me to keep moving forward with the goal of publishing this book.

I am grateful to many families and individuals who have allowed me to share their personal stories of grief. The names, stories and quotations in this book fall into three categories: factual stories and citations with the actual names provided; actual stories with pseudonym provided; and stories that have an actual basis in fact but with some of the details and names altered. To all of these individuals, I express appreciation and the hope that their story of grief will be helpful to those who read this book.

Preface

EVERYONE DIES. EVERY FAMILY grieves. There is no other pastoral challenge as universal as death. This truth is so simple and powerful that medieval churches often displayed vivid images of *Danse Macabre*, the Dance of Death. In stained glass windows, tapestries or murals, a skeletal or sometimes a dark-robed grim reaper moved through the world calling everyone of every age and social status.

Today, no American church architect would propose decorating with *Danse Macabre*. People are terrified of admitting that we are aging, let alone dying. Before I became Editor of *ReadTheSpirit* magazine and books, I was a journalist who specialized in reporting on religious issues for newspapers. One year, I worked with a team of investigative reporters studying every family who visited Dr. Jack Kevorkian for assistance in suicide. We found that some families were so terrified of an agonizing death that a mere diagnosis of a scary disorder drove a loved one to suicide. The greater tragedy we uncovered in our reporting was that, in some instances, the dead man or woman was misdiagnosed and had years to live. They rushed to end their lives out of the sheer terror of contemplating a slower death. What happened after these deaths? None of the Kevorkian families were convicted of a crime, of course, but their reactions to these deaths were so intense that many families found themselves locked in a prison of grief. Yes, Kevorkian and his clients do represent an extreme response to death and grief. But they also illustrate the depth of the American anxiety concerning all things having to do with death.

In his new book, *Guide for Grief*, the Rev. Dr. Rodger Murchison describes how easily all families—ordinary families like yours and mine—can fall into negative patterns of grief. Of course, grief is not only natural, it is essential. Grief is both a painful and a healthy part of life.

"Grief is the price we pay for love," Queen Elizabeth II told the world after the terrorist attacks on 9/11/2001. Right now, 1 in 3 American households includes a person who is a full-time caregiver for someone with a chronic and, in many cases, a life-threatening condition. The American population is aging at a relentless rate as baby boomers finally confront their own mortality. All of us who love will grieve—and our grief may run far longer than many of our friends will understand. We all need help in exploring the universal journey of grief.

This guide takes a Christian approach to death and grieving. That's the religious affiliation voiced by 4 out of 5 Americans, according to research by the Pew Forum on Religion and Public Life. Families who are not Christian also will benefit from these basic, well-tested principles, which Rodger Murchison has gleaned from ancient traditions as well as the latest scholarly research into coping with grief.

—*David Crumm, General Editor*

(David Crumm is the founding editor of *ReadTheSpirit.com*, an online magazine, and of *ReadTheSpirit Books*. David is a journalist with more than 30 years of experience who served as General Editor for this book.)

Introduction

TIMOTHY OFTEN TOOK A lawn chair to the cemetery to sit by Sally's grave and talk to her. He'd tell her what he had been doing and how much he loved her. He often left the cemetery in tears. They had been married 32 years. Two years after her death, Timothy still grieved her loss. The grief was understandable—even the frequent cemetery visits. Then, I discovered that he broke off every new relationship in his life and his cemetery visits were a time when he cleansed himself of the guilt he felt for allowing new friends into his life. Something was wrong. Timothy was stuck in grief.

Millions of people seek out pastors and other counselors after the loss of loved ones, asking for help in moving through their journey with grief. Most stories are not as unusual as Timothy's. Sometimes, people find themselves stuck in other phases of grief. After a heartbreaking loss, many people lash out in anger at God—a normal part of the grieving process—but some turn this anger into a mantra of woe. Their anger at God over their loss can spill into every area of their lives.

While the process of grieving varies widely, it does follow predictable patterns for most people. When the progression toward healing is obstructed, people need help in getting unstuck.

Most people have heard that there are "stages" to grief, typically referring to Elisabeth Kübler-Ross' landmark five-stage process: denial, anger, bargaining, depression and acceptance. But most people are unaware of the ever-growing body of research into grief. There are other ways of describing and engaging with the predictable patterns of grief. There are many well-tested techniques that can be helpful. A person who is stuck in grief may be assuming that Kübler-Ross' five phases are set in stone—a staircase out of grief chiseled out for everyone in all situations. If they find themselves looping back through phases, or skipping others, they may become discouraged that they are not correctly marching up the steps. We can make a big difference in people's lives simply by helping families understand that there are various models for grief and our journey is not as clear-cut as climbing a staircase.

Because many people fear aging and dread the inevitable truth of death, few of us learn about or prepare for the end that comes to all of us. Professionals have developed a wide array of counseling techniques to help people move through this universal journey of grief. In this book, I explain a number of these techniques for general readers—such as "reframing." Using this technique, people are invited to focus on their loss from a fresh perspective. This does not bring our loved one back to life. What changes are the ways we look at our loss, understand the loss and respond to the loss. Just as a painting takes on new dimensions when given a new frame, people who reframe their grief can discover new sources of strength.

This example of reframing is both a wise psychological practice and a truth deeply rooted in scripture. The author of Hebrews tells us: "If they had been thinking of that land from which they had gone out, they would have had opportunity to return. But as it is, they desired a better country." (*Hebrews 11:15-16*) Instead of bemoaning the loss of comforts in their previous land (as the Moses-led Israelites did many years later), the writer of Hebrews is telling us that Abraham's people trusted that God was leading and blessing them. For Abraham, the "promised land" was more than a new place in which to dwell, it was also a reality of mind and heart—reframing life in the belief that God had called him to a significant new life. Traumatic moments not only change people's lives, but they change people's views of God, of themselves and of life. Rather than battling to resist those changes, reframing frees a person to grow through them. Abraham understood that timeless truth—although he obviously did not coin the term we use today to describe it.

After the death of his wife, C.S. Lewis wrote poignantly in his book, *A Grief Observed*, "I thought I could make a map of sorrow. Sorrow, however, … needs not a map but a history." What Lewis learned is that grief painfully opens up our lives to fresh insights about our past and fresh hopes for the future. We mourn our loss, but grief also leads us to new vistas.

Guide for Grief is designed to nudge these grief travelers in healthy directions, tested through the millennia by people of faith and undergirded by years of research into identifying and teaching these techniques to men and women. You will find cutting-edge scholarship referenced throughout this book—and a list of recommended readings from those scholars at the end of this book. You also will find helpful references from scripture. In these chapters, I suggest many techniques you can use—and I close each chapter with a prayer, inviting you to join me in these prayers. I suggest you print them out and place them on your dinner table, fold them into a frequently read book or hang them in your home as a reminder.

Over time, you will find more resources at http://www.GuideForGrief.info. Those resources include a small-group study guide plus suggestions of helpful organizations and websites. Although many people fear death, congregational leaders will discover that organizing a small-group series on this book—or the formation of a grief-support group—will prove to be a potent outreach program in your community.

We welcome your ideas and questions on our website. I look forward to hearing from you there.

—*Rodger B. Murchison*

Safe Journey

CHAPTER 1

What Happens When We Die?

FEW OF US UNDERSTAND very much about life, so how are we expected to understand anything about death? This ultimate mystery of all mysteries is waiting for everyone—and our response to the reality of death can alter the way we grieve and the way we live the rest of our lives.

The Bible gives us some clues about the understanding of death and what is awaiting us after we die. The apostle Paul tells the Corinthians we will all be changed at death. Paul encourages the faithful with the hope of resurrection. He explains that our earthly bodies will be changed to spiritual bodies. It will happen in the "twinkling of an eye," as the trumpet sounds and death is swallowed up in victory. And who gives us this victory? Jesus Christ the Lord. (1 Corinthians 15:35-58)

In my own ministry, I have helped many families cope with grief—and I have heard countless stories about the way grief changes our lives. In this book, I will share some of those stories that may help you wrestle with these common challenges. I have protected the identities of families by changing many of the names, but all of these stories are true. Here is the first one:

Rachel and Bert were married for 62 years. After Bert died, Rachel began to go to the cemetery every week. Then sometimes she would go twice a week or more. She would stare at the gravestone and, so no one could hear, she would quietly tell Bert how much she loved and missed him. When Rachel was asked why she did this, she explained that the cemetery was where they put Bert and she wanted to be with him.

Cemetery visits can be very important and helpful in our grief. At the gravesite, we often feel reconnected with our deceased loved one. But, here is a caution concerning cemetery visits: Grief frequently will pull us from the reality of the present to a surreal place that thwarts and distorts healthy grief. During cemetery visits, be mindful of the need for remembering the past but be equally attentive to the need for living in the reality of the present and hoping for the future.

In Luke 24, angels said to the women at Jesus' tomb, "Why seek the living among the dead? He is not here, he has risen." This resurrection story of Jesus is good news to my friend Rachel who is in a desperate search for Bert, the love of her life. Of course, Bert already has found the answer to the question about what happens when we die. God designed a divine plan by which humanity will inherit eternity—the plan is resurrection.

One of the most dramatic stories of resurrection is found in John 11:17-27. These verses are commonly known as "The Raising of Lazarus," yet bringing Lazarus back to life was not the real miracle. The focus of the story is revealed in verse 25, where Jesus says, "I am the resurrection and the life." For those who grieve the loss of a loved one, this text can reassure them that Jesus has power over life and death. Throughout this book, I have adapted a number of passages from the King James Version of the Bible to make them easier for contemporary readers. Here is a portion of that story from John 11:

Then Martha said to Jesus: "Lord, if you had been here, my brother would not have died. But I know that even now, whatever you ask God—God will give it to you."

Jesus said to her: "Your brother will rise again."

Martha said to him: "I know he shall rise again in the resurrection at the last day."

Jesus said to her: "Martha, I am the resurrection, and the life. He who believes in me, though he were dead, now he shall live; and whoever lives and believes in me shall never die. Do you believe this?"

Martha said to him: "Yes, Lord. I believe you are the Christ, the Son of God, who has come into the world."

There is comfort in knowing that our loved one has been resurrected to a new life. There is strength in knowing that the same Lord that secures new life after death is available to us to secure new life during and after grief. Remember Jesus words: "I am the resurrection and the life."

Writer and educator Henry van Dyke wrote poetry and hymns, including "Joyful, Joyful We Adore Thee" set to Beethoven's music. Among van Dyke's best-remembered short poems is *Parable of Immortality*:

I am standing upon the seashore.
A ship at my side spreads her white sails to the morning breeze
and starts for the blue ocean.
She is an object of beauty and strength,
and I stand and watch until at last she hangs
like a speck of white cloud
just where the sea and sky come down to mingle with each other.
Then someone at my side says,

"There she goes!"
Gone where?
Gone from my sight . . . that is all.
She is just as large in mast and hull and spar
as she was when she left my side
and just as able to bear her load of living freight
to the place of destination.
Her diminished size is in me, not in her.
And just at the moment
when someone at my side says,
"There she goes! "
There are other eyes watching her coming . . .
and other voices ready to take up the glad shout . . .
"Here she comes! "

Rachel, my cemetery friend, needed to hear encouraging words like van Dyke's and the promises of resurrection hope through Jesus Christ. The promise for Bert was life everlasting in heaven with God. The promise for Rachel was life on earth during and after grief. Jesus was telling Rachel: I am the life, if you have faith in me, you do not have to die in your grief.

This new life in Jesus, for Bert and Rachel, required what grief specialist J. William Worden calls "relocation." The definition of this concept is: "withdrawing emotional energy from the deceased and reinvesting it in another relationship" or "finding an appropriate place for the dead in the (emotional) life of the mourner." Those words may seem harsh when you first read them, but Worden is not suggesting that you simply forget your deceased loved one. "Reinvesting it in another relationship" does not mean getting remarried or somehow trying to replace the deceased with a new relationship. Worden is suggesting that as those who grieve channel emotional energy into healthy living relationships, whatever they may be, the work of appropriate grieving will take place. I saw relocation happen in a powerful way through the relationship of Timothy and Sally:

Two years after Sally died, her husband Timothy was going to the cemetery multiple times a week to be with her. They had been married for 32 years. He wanted to begin other relationships with friends at work and church. The difficulty was that every time he began to enjoy himself in these relationships he would feel guilty. The memory of Sally would overcome Timothy to the point that he would break off every new relationship.

In a Grief Ministry Workshop session, it was suggested to Timothy that he write a letter to Sally. The letter would be an expression of his faithful love and deep appreciation for their relationship and his desire to have the freedom to welcome other relationships. Timothy did write this letter and he took it to the cemetery and read it in front of Sally's grave. After reading the letter, he burned it as an act of letting go and a symbol of relocation.

Here is a piece of wisdom commonly taught in such workshops: If we don't let our loved ones die, they won't let us live. Some people become so obsessed with life in the past that they deprive themselves of the potential of life the way it could be.

What happens when we die? Many people in grief want to know about heaven. Where is it? What is it? Will we have the same relationships in heaven that we have on earth? One widow told me that, for her, heaven had to be one big date with her departed husband. There are several scriptures that give us hints of heaven: Read 2 Corinthians 5:1-5, Philippians 3:20-21 and Matthew 22:23-33, a passage where Jesus explains that people will neither marry nor be given in marriage in heaven.

Whatever it is, heaven will probably be a glorious surprise. C. S. Lewis suggests that what is really wrong with fashionable concepts of happy reunions in heaven is not just the earthbound pictures , but that we make an end out of what is really only a by-product of the true End. Death is as much an entrance as it is an exit. Death is not a wall—it is a doorway. It is only in seeking and longing for God that we discover all our desires truly will find their fulfillment in God. We may think that we want a continuation of our current life, transported to some heavenly realm, but C.S. Lewis and others suggest: We are yearning for far more. Understanding the spiritual dynamics of death can help those who grieve cope with their loss. Death changes our lives, but it does not need to destroy the living left behind.

> A grieving widow, Mary, asked if it were possible for the living to communicate with the dead. She said sometimes she would fondly remember her husband and could hear his voice. She found herself trying to have a conversation with him. Mary said it was not like using a séance or a medium. She just yearned to speak with him again and felt that she almost could.

When I heard Mary's story, I told her this is a normal reaction to grief. Some people will speak to the dead verbally; some will speak sub-vocally. For a brief time following the death of our loved ones, communication can be therapeutic. We continue to feel a connection to the deceased. But as I mentioned earlier in the case of Timothy and Sally, sometimes that communication can become unhealthy. Timothy told me on many occasions that he would bring a lawn chair to the cemetery and sit in front of Sally's gravestone and talk with her. This went on for more than two years. His need to communicate with his deceased wife had become detrimental to the normal grief process.

A positive faith response to this desire to communicate with our departed loved ones is found in Hebrews 12:1: "Therefore, given that we are surrounded by so great a cloud of witnesses, let us lay aside every weight and the sin that overwhelms us, and let us run with patience the race that is set before us. ..." The context of this verse is the writer of Hebrews describing the meaning of faith. The text gives a sweeping history of the biblical faithful and how each generation depended on God. Now this great cloud of witnesses surrounds us, the writer tells us. In a spiritual way, our deceased loved ones are these witnesses and they are encouraging us in our grief, in our faith and in our life.

What if our loved one is not a Christian? What happens when they die? Norma's parents died several years ago. Neither of them were Christians. This is the question she asked me: "I think my parents believed in God but in their own unusual way. We never discussed religion and the only way the name of Jesus was ever spoken in our home was as a curse. I've often wondered if I'm grieving for them on earth, or am I really grieving the dread that I've lost them to eternity. Have I?"

It is neither my place nor Norma's to judge the spiritual condition of her parents, but the fact that Norma does have some ambivalence about her parents' eternal destiny exacerbates the pain of grief. There is a wide range of teaching about these issues within Christianity, but I have found it most helpful to remind people that God doesn't call us to make such judgments, thank goodness. In his thought-provoking little book, *The Great Divorce*, C. S. Lewis provides one imaginary vision of heaven and hell that suggests people choose what amounts to hell by their willful decision to avoid God. But we need not live in fear. In Lewis' book, God eternally reaches out in loving ways. The apostle Paul reminded the Thessalonians in I Thessalonians 4:13-14 that Jesus and the hope of resurrection answer our questions of what happens at death. Jesus broke loose from the grave, and God through Christ will bring new life to all who die in Him.

Henry van Dyke's poem about the ship is a beautiful picture of death. Eternity is before us and God Almighty, the creator of heaven and earth, is sovereign over all. Grief is the price we pay for love and van Dyke wrote about that process in lines that are still repeated and even sung today: "Time is too slow for those who wait, too swift for those who fear, too long for those who grieve, too short for those who rejoice, but for those who love—time is eternity."

Closing Prayer

Dear God of Heaven and Earth:
Eternity seems so far away.
My arms ache for touch.
My ears beg for sound.
My eyes yearn for a glance.
Where is my loved one, Lord?
Death has taken away a part of me, but where?
O God of Heaven and Earth:
Remind my troubled soul that
You are sovereign over this world and the next.
May that be enough to satisfy my anxious heart
when I long for love's embrace
until I truly find my rest in Thee.
Through Jesus Christ we pray.
Amen

Resurrection Hope

CHAPTER 2

How Do I Live Without My Loved One?

"HOW DO I GO on?" So many people have uttered these words after the death of a loved one. There is no easy answer, yet we must talk about this question and find a way forward. If we do not deal with grief, then grief will deal with us. The effect of unresolved grief can be devastating for the loved one who is left alive.

> "Bob and I got married when I was 18. Doing life with him is all I can remember. How do I live without Bob?" That's how Rita asked the question after their 55 years of marriage ended with Bob's death. For the last few years, Rita had been even more than Bob's wife—she had been his caregiver. She had organized her daily routine around Bob and his needs. How could her life go on?

We can remind Rita of passages like 1 Thessalonians 4:13-14: "But I would not have you be uninformed, my friends, concerning those who are already dead. You should not be weighed down in grief, like those who have no hope. For if we believe that Jesus died and rose again, God will bring back to life those who believe in Jesus."

But Rita's life has changed forever. In working with grief, we encounter lessons like: "Weep softly, but grieve long;" and hear warnings such as: "We live in a society that doesn't educate us to deal with loss but rather teaches us how to acquire and hold on to things." Death and grief are struggles for which millions of people—people just like you and me and our families—are poorly prepared. Death brings about one of the most dramatic changes of all for the survivors. Our grieving should not be ignored because this is a process that shapes the rest of our lives. Wise words alone are not enough. That's why an intentional process of dealing with grief sometimes is called "grief work."

The sorrow of grief and its duration are frequently related to the extent to which those who mourn focus on the work of grief. Grief work is often defined in stages or processes. Because people grieve in different ways, the manner in which people move through the grief journey is also different. It is important to keep in mind that these grief stages and processes are not sequential or linear. People tend to move through the grief process in a cyclical pattern. For some, the bereavement process falls into overlapping phases. A mourner may move from one phase to another and later experience an earlier phase again. Some will not experience one or more of the grief phases at all. The hope is, as mourners do their grief work, they discover they are moving forward to a positive resolution of their feelings of grief.

Elizabeth Kübler-Ross was a pioneer in trying to chart the phases of grief. She identified five grief stages:

1. Denial
2. Anger
3. Bargaining
4. Depression

5. Acceptance

However, that is not the only model for understanding grief. Dr. Colin Parkes is a psychiatrist honored by Queen Elizabeth II for his many contributions to grieving people and the professionals who care for them. Dr. J. William Worden is a professor of psychology who also is internationally known for his work on bereavement, including research at Harvard and other universities. Parkes and Worden have charted the course of grief in new ways—one describing the "process of grief" and the other writing about the "tasks of grief." A friend of mine, Dr. Joy S. Berger who directs the Hospice Institute in Louisville, Kentucky, has brought Parkes' and Worden's multifaceted dynamics of grief together in the following table:

Processes (Parkes) and Tasks (Worden)

1. Process: Numbness, shock and denial
   Task: To accept the reality of the loss
2. Process: Yearning, painful, longing, searching
   Task: To work through to the pain of grief
3. Process: Disorganization and despair
   Task: To adjust to an environment in which the deceased is missing
4. Process: Reorganization
   Task: To emotionally relocate the deceased and move on with life

These terms are a good summary of their conclusions, adapted here so that we can think about their ideas side by side. Parkes does not use the specific term "reorganization," but he writes "it is only after the stage of disorganization that recovery occurs." Considering their insights together like this, we see that Parkes and Worden are charting similar movements through grief. They are showing us that grief is a journey that takes time and work—but there is, indeed, a pathway through grief so that we eventually can go on with life even after a devastating loss.

Though the first are self-explanatory, the second, third and fourth tasks suggested by Worden need some clarification. In the second task, it is important for those who have lost a loved one to realize that grief work is painful and should not be avoided. A person should not try to suppress this pain or the grief process could be prolonged. In the third task, the survivors are usually not aware of all the roles that were played by the deceased. Adjusting to the environment means discovering and coping with all of these roles that are now missing—some of which need to be filled. In the fourth task, grieving people realize the loved one is gone and allow that departed person to move to a new location in their minds and memories. We are not "forgetting" them; we are making room for our lives to continue.

Naturally, the aim of the grief journey is resolution, acceptance, and affirmation of life in spite of the loss—but there are no shortcuts. Unfortunately, our culture is so goal-oriented and competitive that reaching the final stage of grief is a preoccupation. Many people rush the process or friends push them. I call this malady "McGrief Syndrome." We rush through the grief process as we would a fast-food takeout window, desperately striving for some elusive Kübler-Ross final stage of "Acceptance." We do not take into account the slow and unpredictable nature of this process in which we may loop through various phases yet may never experience all of them.

Sören Kierkegaard's "weep softly, but grieve long" stands in distinct contrast to the idea of setting up goalposts in grieving. The 19th-century theologian argued that we should grieve for our beloved until we too shall die. Rather than putting the loss behind us, Kierkegaard would have us embrace it and permit our grief to strengthen our relationship with God. Kierkegaard's approach has much merit but we need to encourage those who grieve to understand the difference between appropriately embracing the memory of the deceased and inappropriately becoming fixated on the deceased.

All of these approaches that I have summarized may have merit for you and your family. Grieving is neither as universal nor as clear-cut as a 5-step Kübler-Ross checklist.

I first heard the story of Rachel and Bert, which appears in Chapter 1, during a workshop that I was leading. Rachel wanted and needed to move on with her life. So, we talked about her children and her grandchildren. I encouraged her to refocus her attention on these living members of her family. Bert surely would have wanted that. But the question continues to echo within millions of families: How do I live without my loved one?

As men and women deliberately work through grief, they begin to realize that grief is a part of life. Grief is not the enemy. Grief is like breathing air and drinking water. If you live, you are going to grieve.

Closing Prayer

Dear God of Life:
How can I go on?
Living without my loved one is so painful.
My grief is sometimes unbearable.
I want to scream!
Cry out!
Am I going crazy?
O God of Life:
Rescue me from the land of death.
Pull away the shroud that drapes my life.
Send Your Son of Light to push away the darkness.
I lean my mournful soul on
Your everlasting arms of Hope.
You have set my loved one free for all eternity.
Set me free, too.
In Jesus' name.
Amen

The Valley of life

CHAPTER 3

Are There Healthy and Unhealthy Ways to Grieve?

PEOPLE GRIEVE IN SO many different ways that declaring some healthy, and others unhealthy, is presumptuous. Grief is personal. Professional grief therapists tell us that there are exceptions, but healthy or normal grief follows a somewhat predictable pattern as described in the last chapter. Terms such as unhealthy or abnormal grief refer to individuals who are overwhelmed by loss and remain in an intense state of grief without progressing toward resolution. This is commonly referred to as a person who is "stuck" in grief, or "stuck" in a stage or phase of grief such as: denial, anger, depression, guilt, loneliness, fatigue or helplessness. Unhealthy grief can be damaging; therefore, individuals who feel they are experiencing abnormal grief should contact a professional counselor.

Healthy grief often involves faith. When a loved one dies, it is natural for people to question their faith. Some of these questions may have been in the mind of the person long before this time of bereavement—but in response to grief, these questions become more urgent. In workshops, I teach: Allow your faith to inform your grief, and allow your grief to inform your faith. Of course, this is a timeless truth. In Matthew 5:4, Jesus teaches: "Blessed are they that mourn for they shall be comforted." In *Amazing Grace*, John Newton writes: "Through many dangers, toils and snares I have already come, tis grace hath brought me safe thus far, and grace will lead me home."

Does faith make grieving easier and healthier? Not necessarily! Some people assume that, if you are a Christian, your faith will automatically provide an advantage during the grief process. They might quote 1 Thessalonians 4:13-14:

> But I would not have you be uninformed, my friends, concerning those who are already dead. You should not be weighed down in grief, like those who have no hope. For if we believe that Jesus died and rose again, God will bring back to life those who believe in Jesus.

One interpretation of these verses is to affirm that those who are Christians will find grief more endurable, but this assumption has an obvious flaw. Paul affirms that Christians "should not" grieve like others who are not Christians because Christians do have hope in Christ. But the issue is: Will the Christian recognize the hope that is available? Will the Christian be able to grasp that hope? In the face of grief, Christians may not relate their faith to their grief. There are many reasons Christians might not utilize faith during grief:

- The mourner may be so overwhelmed with grief that he or she cannot think clearly about anything, especially their faith.
- God is often the target of a mourner's anger.
- An immature faith might be unable to bear the weight of grief.

- You never know how much you really believe anything until its truth or falsehood becomes a matter of life and death to you.

There is an even larger issue at work: Grief can and should change aspects of our faith as we move through it—which is not a pleasant process. I am not saying that anyone's faith was "wrong" or needed to be "fixed" before a loved one's death. We are talking here about a truth that affects us all: Faith should always be growing, maturing and evolving. Faith is not a static thing that we once appropriate and never alter. Faith is active, living, changing and always seeking God in new places. Grief is one of those occasions in life when we begin to assess who we are and what we believe. It is very appropriate for us to question ourselves, to question God, to stretch our faith, and search for new horizons of truth. The following four people have shared their thoughts about faith and grief:

- Sue's response to death: "When my sister was killed— murdered—I did not lose my faith but I did redefine it. I began to question my prior belief system that did not deal very well with death and tragedy. You can only believe in the God you can conceive of. As your concept of God changes, then for you—He changes." Sue is allowing her grief to shape her faith and risking the uncertainty of a faith exposed to reevaluation.

- Barbara, who is 66, expresses a similar feeling: "Grief has forced me to test my beliefs and come up with a more realistic belief system. Negative happenings can have positive impact on how you live your life. The God I now believe in is different from the God I believed in at 30. He is different from the God I believed in before my husband died. I wonder who has changed?" Barbara's faith has been strengthened because she has allowed her grief to profoundly influence her life. This is a healthy way to grieve.

- Don makes a different assumption: "If Christians respond to grief in a bad way, or a negative way, that means that their faith before the loved one's death was not what it should be."
- Mary has the same kind of assumption: "Yes, if someone is having trouble, then their faith is weak. I link my own weak days emotionally with my faith. If my faith was as strong as it should be, I should accept the fact that it was time for my husband to die. But there are moments when I cannot accept it and that is not good. My mother tells me to trust God."

As Don and Mary illustrate, not everyone feels that grief is an occasion for faith development. They perceive a cause-and-effect relationship between grief and faith: Strong faith should produce a mature grief response; weak faith makes for an immature response. Their comments assume that faith is static and that grief should not prompt fresh questions about our beliefs. This cause-and-effect theology becomes a self-centered conviction that the purpose of faith is simply to get us through events in life in predetermined ways. But faith is much more than that. Faith is not an independent act of our will to believe that something should be a certain way. We are drawn toward faith by our humbling awareness of God, an Infinite Being. Remember Sue's remark? "You can only believe in the God you can conceive of." In the end, Sue concludes, "I did not lose my faith but I did redefine it." In contrast to Sue's acceptance of new insights in her faith, Mary wants to compel her static faith to make sense of her husband's death and neatly sort out her feelings of grief—an unrealistic expectation. That is unhealthy grieving.

God can use our grief as revelation. If faith is a dynamic part of our daily lives, then our faith changes and grows as new chapters in life are written. Grief is no different than other significant passages in life, such as one's initial religious experience, marriage or the birth of a child. But, grief will have minimal influence if our faith is cloistered away and we strive to seem unaffected by the experiences of life. Grief invites our ship of faith to sail for new horizons and only those whose ships have left the harbor will ever discover what is possible on this challenging voyage.

A technique for allowing grief and faith to mutually influence each other is "reframing." This technique encourages the bereaved to look at the circumstances of their loved one's death from a new perspective. In this book's Introduction, I offered the example of Abraham's dramatic reframing of his life and faith. In my own life, I have experienced this truth. When my father died, I often was plagued by negative thoughts like these:

> God, look at what I have lost! I can't call Dad on the phone; can't ask him for advice. He won't see my children graduate from high school or college or get married.

I don't know what finally helped me to "reframe" my grief. I give God the credit. Instead of focusing on what I had lost, I began to say:

> God, look at what I gained in life thanks to my wonderful Dad! He was a good father, a good husband to my mother, involved in community and church activities. What a blessing that I knew him at all!

In reframing my grief, or looking at my grief from a new perspective, I did not change the fact that my father was dead. What changed was the way in which I understood my father's death. For people of faith, reframing involves allowing our faith to inform our grief and allowing our grief to inform our faith. The idea is as old as Abraham and as new as the latest research into grief.

Are there healthy and unhealthy ways to grieve? Of course there are, but each person's life history and faith history is different; thus each person's grief experience is different. You may have heard a surviving spouse tell you something like this:

I would like to describe my grief in just a few words—but I can't. Grief isn't one thing, one feeling, one moment. Grief is a journey with disappointments and revelations all along the way. There are twists and turns. Sometimes I feel lost. Sometimes I circle back. I am discouraged some days. I will admit that I have been angry some days. But then—I turn a corner and God reveals a totally new landscape.

For many, healthy grief does not begin after a loved one dies. My fellow church member Jimmy Smith tells me, "We can better deal with grief after death, if we prepare for grief before death." He suggests that we talk with our loved ones about death and grief. Do things with family and loved ones while they are alive and then we don't regret missed opportunities after they die. My friend, Dr. Allan Josephson, once shared this healthy response to grief: "Even after a loved one's death, we can learn from our grief and loss to heighten our appreciation of the present."

Closing Prayer

Dear Source of all my faith:
Sometimes I feel so confused.
I want to believe You are my comfort and hope
but my sorrow is overwhelming.
This long valley of grief is lonely and frightening.
Where is the faith I so desperately need?
Dear Source of all my faith,
walk beside me.
When I stumble,
may I know Your strength.
Steady my step.
Surprise me with new vistas.
Help me carry the load until my journey's end.

Through the love that will not let us go, we pray.
Amen

My God, my God, why have you forsaken me?

S. Pollock

CHAPTER 4

Why Did My Loved One Die?

WHY?

Why did she die?

Why was he taken away from me?

Why do I have to suffer all this pain?

In grief, these are universal questions, but they are not intellectual inquiries. These are pleas from the heart. From deep within our soul, we seek to understand this painful mystery. These are appropriate questions. Ask them! We all do. Ask family members, friends, ministers, doctors and anyone you trust enough to ask. Then, remember this caution concerning "why" questions: We must ask these questions, but in the end they do not satisfy. After you have exhausted every form of "why," you probably will discover that "why" is a one-way road to nowhere. We cannot solve this mystery.

When you reach that point in your inquiry, I suggest changing the question from "why" to the more practical "what." What do we do, now that this has happened? What can be done that would honor the memory of the deceased? What can be done for the sake of the ones who grieve? By posing this new kind of question, we open ourselves to a world of possibilities—possibilities that can be extremely healing to a hurting heart.

"Why" questions express our negative feelings: Why now? Why did someone so good have to die? Why was I not prepared? Why didn't the doctors know? In contrast, "what" questions have so much positive potential: What is my favorite memory? What memories should I preserve, write down, pass along to others? What stories should I tell to children and grandchildren? What kind of life would my loved one want me to have now? By reframing our grief with a different set of questions, we find ourselves moving from death and despair to life and hope.

This was Job's story in the Bible. He had lost everything and began asking God: Why? God let Job voice all his questions—just as God allows all of ours. Questions do not offend God. Yet, God knew finite Job could not understand the Infinite. Ultimately, God also knew that Job really would not have been satisfied with any answer to that question: Why? Here are some excerpts from Job taken from 1:20, 7:20-21, portions of chapter 38 and 42:1-3. As I have done throughout this book, I have paraphrased these texts to make them easier for all readers:

> Then Job got up, tore his robe, shaved his head.
> "Why O God have you made me your target?
> So I have become a burden to myself?
> Why do you not forgive my sin and take away my iniquity?"
> Then, the Lord answered Job out of the whirlwind:
> "Where were you when I laid the foundations of the earth?
> Explain that, if you have understanding!
> On what were its foundations fastened,
> or who laid its cornerstones when the morning stars sang together
> and all the heavenly beings shouted for joy?"
> Then Job was humbled and answered the Lord:

"I know that You can do everything,
and that no thought can be withheld from You.
I have spoken what I did not understand,
things too wonderful for me, which I did not
know."

We are all like Job in the midst of our grief, asking: Why? I encourage you to read and discuss the entire book of Job with friends and perhaps your pastor or Bible study group. Through the years, many contemporary writers and even filmmakers have tried to recapture this ancient story's relevance. Job's story reminds us that, whatever answers we may seek and whatever answers God may provide, there still is a part of us that dies when our loved ones die. Our losses hurt! They hurt deeply! There are not enough answers in the cosmos to bring back those we have lost. Consider this more contemporary story:

> Frank's son Joe died when the boy was twelve. Frank kept a journal and the following was his entry one month after Joe's funeral: "It's Father's Day and I feel like I have lost everything. Everyone keeps telling me how strong I am, how brave I am, but I am tired of hearing it. My work is a mess. My sense of humor—now where is that? Where there was joy, there is pain. Where there was hope, there is fear. Where there was anticipation, there is dread. Nothing can remove this dagger from my heart. Maybe worst of all, I feel like I don't care anymore. Caring was everything, now it is nothing. Happy Father's Day."

Compare Frank's entry with passages from Job and we see that these questions echo down the ages. There is nothing wrong with asking "why"—yet most of us finally discover that grief arrives at no resolution through that query.

My father died of lung cancer in 1994. Why? I found myself asking that again and again. His cancer was diagnosed in June.

The doctor advised no treatment: no chemotherapy, no surgery and no radiation. My father died in August. I was haunted by the question: Why had his doctors missed this for so long? Our doctor admitted that, if the cancer had been detected earlier, then treatments might have been effective. Why had they missed it? I knew my father had regularly visited his doctor. I knew that they had ordered lab work in late 1993 and early 1994. These were talented physicians. Why had they missed it? I grew angry. Why didn't some technician or nurse recognize the signs? Why was our family left with only hospice as a final option? I had no desire to sue my father's doctor for malpractice, but my grief kept angrily repeating: Why? At my father's funeral, cousin Julie sang, "It Is Well with My Soul." But it was not well with my soul. I sat there still asking: Why?

There was no easy resolution. Months passed and still I was stuck on: Why? More than a year passed and someone asked me to look more closely at the lyrics of Horatio Spafford's song, "It Is Well with My Soul." Finally, my eyes fell on these words: "Whatever my lot, Thou has taught me to say, It is well, it is well with my soul." I realized that my grief had paralyzed my ability to see beyond my relentless questioning. Spafford's words reminded me that, even after the death of my father, God could teach me. If I opened myself to God's teaching, then my perspective might change and I might reach the question: What? What am I to do next? Through my faith, after a long and painful journey, my answer became: I can affirm that it is well—it is well with my soul.

Closing Prayer

Creator God:
I have many questions.
I have no answers.
My anger is rising.
Like Job and his friends, I must ask—
Why?

I can't help myself.
Like the Psalmists, I must cry—
Why!?!
Hear me, God of Grace:
Grant me the patience of Job.
Grant me mercy even as my questions churn.
Rescue me.
Sustainer God:
Even in this struggle, lead me.
Reframe me.
What …?
What do you have in store?
Like Paul, I know—
Your peace passes all understanding!
Help me to declare:
It is well with my soul.
Help me to affirm:
It is well.
Amen

God Receiving

CHAPTER 5

Did God Take My Loved One?

IF WE ARE STUCK too long on the question, "Why did my loved one die?" then we may find that query turning into an arrogant demand: "Did God take my loved one!?!" Blaming God for human death is common. But if the question arises in anger and frustration, then we may be arguing against God's ultimate goodness. We may be suggesting that God is somehow complicit in killing our loved one. If you have voiced this question, you are not alone. So many men and women have asked this down through the centuries that an entire branch of theology, called theodicy, is focused on defending God's goodness and power in the face of suffering and death. As we affirmed in the prayer at the close of Chapter 4: God is our Creator and Sustainer. In this chapter, we look at the common tendency to blame God for taking our loved one away from us.

Let's start with what Jesus taught us about God's role when our life on earth is over. John 14 reminds us that God has prepared a place for us. As Jesus explains it:

> In my Father's house are many mansions. If it were not so, I would have told you. I go to prepare

a place for you. And, if I go and prepare a place for you, then I will come again and will receive you to myself—so that where I am, there you may be also.

The word "receive" is a beautiful illustration of divine deliverance. Jesus does not tell us that, in death, God is coming to take or snatch or grab us. Jesus says that God receives us. Envision the loving arms of God embracing us at death, freeing us to experience new life everlasting.

God is good, as many churchgoers affirm regularly. Let me put this in stark terms: God is not a murderer. Christians around the world often proclaim this truth: All the time, God is good. One way to understand this important teaching in relation to death is to realize that God—who is all good and all-powerful—has created humanity for two worlds. In the earthly world, God invites us into relationship with Him through new birth in Jesus Christ. And on earth we also have the opportunity for relationships with others living in God's creation. In the heavenly world, God invites us into a deeper relationship with Him; and death represents the doorway to new birth in that second world God has created and sustains for us.

Still, that image of God receiving us in love is hard to keep clearly in our minds, especially when we are hurting and discouraged. Why would a good God who has all the power in the world not figure out a way to prevent this suffering we feel? Why would a good God allow our loved one to die, perhaps in the prime of life? In writing this chapter, I am not encouraging you to delve deep into your anger. I am acknowledging that anger at God is common and I am recommending we openly discuss these difficult issues. Dr. Granger E. Westberg, a pioneer in grief counseling, warns against encouraging people to embrace such anger. In his classic book, *Good Grief*, Westberg wrote that if these feelings are allowed to dominate a person's life, they can be very harmful. Westberg knew this truth both as a professor of medicine at the University of Chicago and as a Lutheran pastor and professor of religion. We do not want to ignore our anger at God, but we do not want to linger in that grief.

The late Wayne E. Oates was a pioneer like Westberg in researching the most difficult issues in grief. Oates studied at both the Southern Baptist Theological Seminary in Kentucky and Union Theological Seminary in New York City. He eventually taught at the University of Louisville School of Medicine. In his overall research into life's most common crises, Oates is famous for coining the term "workaholic." Throughout his own research, Oates looked at our human relationships from many perspectives. If we experience anger during periods of grief, Oates concluded, that anger is really a secondary feeling that people use against primary feelings they experience such as hopelessness, envy and helplessness. A widower may exclaim in exasperation: "The house is a total wreck! She used to do it all; I feel helpless." Seeing anger as a secondary feeling changes our perspective in helping a grieving person. Perhaps anger is not the crucial issue to confront; perhaps by working through a wider array of conflicting feelings that are surfacing during our grief, the anger will fade.

Often our anger is directed toward others, and if we allow our anger to fester into isolation and estrangement, then it can magnify and prolong our pain. If left unchecked, then feelings of loneliness and abandonment intensify. Here is a common voice of one caught in this particular cycle of grief:

> I am so angry at my sister for her uncaring attitude during our father's illness! I know I need to let it go. It is obviously driving a wedge between the two of us.

Another example arrived in a letter from a friend whose son had recently died:

> My son Sam died at age 19. Not a day goes by that I have not broken down and cried. I tell myself I am blessed to live in a great country, to have loving parents, an adoring wife, and three beautiful

healthy children. I have a good job, a nice house, and live a life that most people would envy. I have been truly blessed. Still, I would rather be a beggar on the street than to have lost my precious Sam. Somehow in his loss, I have learned the true meaning of love.

But, my wife and my parents are mad—mad at God. My mother says she will never forgive Him for taking Sam away from us. To some extent, Sam's death has driven my wife away from the church and God. For some strange reason, it has brought me closer.

What a troubling phrase: "mad—mad at God." Sam's family felt real anger and focused that fury on God. Of course, God understands our anger. Read Psalms if you doubt this truth. Yet, appropriately dealing with anger allows our grief to eventually heal. If anger is understood properly, it can produce a positive transformation.

Remember the prayer that includes these words: "If I should die before I wake, I pray the Lord my soul to take"? This children's prayer took on new meaning as I grieved with Bill and Sue over the loss of their stillborn infant, Baby Jennifer. Here is their story:

> The baby died near the end of Sue's gestation. Her hospital stay was brief. It was a rainy Friday afternoon when Sue and Bill invited me into the family room of their home to plan a funeral. As we discussed the service, they also expressed the pain and anger they both felt.
>
> Sue: "I'm so angry. It hurts! I feel like it hurts all over."
>
> Bill: "I feel much like Sue. I'm confused, I'm mad and I don't understand why this happened. Who is to blame?"

Sue: "I blame God. I prayed to God to get pregnant. I prayed that all would be okay. How could God do this or allow this to happen?"
Angry questions spilled from Sue and Bill: How could God do this? Where was God? As we talked, I held them, cried with them and prayed to God for wisdom and courage.

As time passed, Bill and Sue cried and prayed with me on many other occasions. As the years unfolded, this couple became the proud parents of two healthy children. The family is actively involved in the church. But I have often pondered, that on that rainy Friday afternoon in their family room, their anger toward God could have damaged their faith and driven them away from the church. Instead, they chose to acknowledge their anger and allow God to fashion their faith in a new way.

Over the years, I have heard many metaphors for death that are helpful in understanding this mysterious transition. A friend once told me that he prefers to describe death this way:

A child falls asleep watching television in the family room of her home. The next morning she awakens in her bedroom all comfortable and safe. Her loving father had carried her in his arms from one room of his home to another room of his home. And that, my friend, is dying.

This image mirrors that passage in John 14 so beautifully, it bears repeating: "In my Father's house are many mansions. If it were not so, I would have told you. I go to prepare a place for you. And, if I go and prepare a place for you, then I will come again and will receive you to myself—so that where I am, there you may be also."

We need to be careful, too, with "sleeping" metaphors, because they can scare children. We have all heard stories of families who have experienced problems with children fearfully misunderstanding the old "if-I-should-die-before-I-wake" prayer. But this way of talking about death is a centuries-old tradition in Eastern Orthodox branches of Christianity, where death is typically called "falling asleep in the Lord." An Orthodox memorial service for the departed may include this timeless prayer: "For You O Lord are the Resurrection, the Life, and the Repose of your servant who has fallen asleep."

How do we reach such a deep and confident faith in God's goodness? In the Bible, the book of Ruth tells the epic story of Naomi and her family. This is a powerful saga of grief, anger, resentment and restoration. For one who mourns, especially a widow, the book of Ruth can reveal insights into the experience of grief. In the opening verses, Elimelech and his wife Naomi face a famine in the land of Judah. Together with their two sons, they move to Moab. Soon after, Elimelech dies and the sons marry Moabite women: one named Orpah and one named Ruth. Ten years later, the sons die. Naomi's response to her grief is bitterness and pain. Why did God take her loved ones? Naomi angrily answers: "The Lord has turned against me!" She boldly points her finger at God as the source of her misfortune. Here is my rendering of selected verses from the first chapter of Ruth as Naomi turns her head toward her homeland once again:

> The Almighty has dealt with me so bitterly. I went
> out full and the Lord has brought me home empty.
> Do not call me Naomi! Call me Mara, because the
> Lord has afflicted me; the Almighty has brought
> misfortune upon me.

The contrast between the old name Naomi, meaning pleasant or sweet, and the new name Mara, meaning bitter or sad, points out that Naomi has allowed grief to transform her entire life. Of course, as Bible readers know, Ruth eventually embodies hope for Naomi. Their friendship is exemplified in Ruth's familiar plea: "I beg you not to leave me. Wherever you go, I will go." Faith in human relationships can be a pathway back to a renewed faith in God. It is important to develop and nurture friendships throughout all of life but especially during one's grief. Friends can help us keep a proper perspective. Grief often clouds our perceptions. As painful feelings pile up in our grief, as Oates taught us, they can overflow in anger and further isolate us from the very people we need around us. Frequent conversations with a mature friend can help to restore our balance. When an angry, grieving friend tells us to go away—think of Ruth's response to Naomi, "Wherever you go, I will go."

Closing Prayer

Dear God of Ruth and Naomi:
With Naomi, I have to say—
I am angry, too.
Life is just not fair.
This death is such a waste.
I started out so full of life; now my life seems empty.
Did You take my loved one?
Couldn't You have spared just this one life?
Couldn't You have spared me this pain?
And then, with Ruth, I have to say—
Embrace me in Your loving arms of hope and security.
No, O Lord, I am not going anywhere.
Remind me of the blessing of the friends and loved ones who still surround me.
Remind me that, through our faith in resurrection, there will be glad reunions yet to come.
One day, You will receive me, too.
Until that blessed day, hold safe my loved one gone.
When my journey ends, receive me unto them and Thee.
With Ruth, I pray—
Wherever You go, I will go.

Through Jesus Christ we pray.
Amen

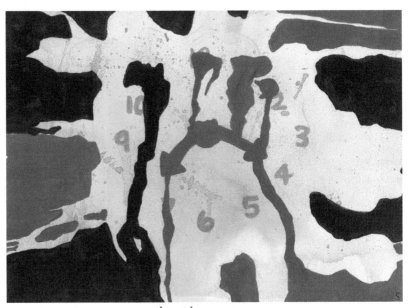

A Time to Mourn

CHAPTER 6

How Long Will My Grief Hurt?

How long will You forget me, O Lord?
Will you forget me forever?
How long will you hide your face from me?
How long will my soul be in pain, having sorrow in
my heart every day?

These are troubling questions from a person painfully struggling with all the emotions we have described so far in this book. Do these questions sound like someone you know? They may. They were voiced thousands of years ago by the writer of Psalm 13. And that writer certainly was not alone. In Psalm 6 we read:

Have mercy on me, O Lord, for I am weak;
O Lord, heal me, for my bones are in pain.
My soul is in grief.
How long, O lord, how long?

Ecclesiastes promises us that there is relief, season by season: "A time to weep, and a time to laugh; a time to mourn, and a time to dance." But when we are in the midst of grief—it hurts! It's painful! Our hurt comes in various forms:

- Physical: Our body senses the ache and trauma of grief.
- Psychological: Our mind seems disoriented and confused.
- Emotional: Our feelings are on edge and often irrational.
- Social: Our relationships with others have changed.
- Spiritual: Our faith may experience profound challenge.

Because grief is frequently upsetting and may seem endless, we tend to avoid our responsibilities in grief. We may give up on active involvement in grief work, but we must persevere. We must keep working day by day. Perhaps this sounds like simple advice. It's not. Consider the experiences of my friend Janice:

> Janice's mother died of cancer at the age of 84. During her final six years of life, Janice had been her caregiver with all of the endless demands that caregiving requires. Then, four months after she buried her mother, Janice's 32-year-old daughter, Cindy, died suddenly of a brain hemorrhage, leaving behind Cindy's husband and two small children. Janice's pain was almost more than she could bear. She was just beginning to deal with some of the issues concerning her mother's death and now this new tragedy had struck! Janice felt numb. She completely shut down her grief work altogether.

Janice's grief was complex and compounded. It was important for her to face one matter at a time because she was overwhelmed with a flood of anxiety. I encouraged Janice to continue working step by step, knowing that the intensity of the pain and longevity of her grief were strongly related to the amount of energy she put into the grief process. Eventually—and this slow process took four years—Janice told me she felt some peace. We talked just after one Christmas, a season that sometimes is difficult for grieving people. But that Christmas seemed to serve as an epiphany in Janice's life that year. She moved through her pain, to her grief.

How long will your grief hurt? Most grief specialists are extremely hesitant to place a timeline on the grief process. J. William Worden, who I introduced in Chapter 2, suggests that, if the person we lose is closely related, then we should be suspicious of any full resolution of grief that takes under a year. For many, Worden advises, two years is not too long. One standard of completed grief work is when the mourner is able to think of the deceased without feeling pain.

It is important for the mourner to remember that although no one welcomes grief, grief itself is not the enemy. The definition of grief is our response to loss. People grieve for all kinds of reasons: loss of a loved one to death, loss of health, loss of job, loss of relationships, infertility, separation, infidelity, divorce, spiritual crisis, retirement—on and on. Grief is like breathing air and drinking water. If you are going to live, then you are going to grieve.

How long will my grief hurt? The hurt of grief is often intensified by the source of our pain.

Sources of Grief Pain

- **Sadness.** Most mourners experience a sensation of sadness or melancholy. We feel that life is heavy and a weight is pressing against the body.
- **Anger.** The feeling of anger is one of the most confusing emotions for the bereaved. The focus of anger varies: for the deceased, for oneself, the medical profession, the clergy, other family members and even God. Some mourners are angry and cannot identify the direction of this anger. One suicide survivor told

me she was so very angry with her deceased husband. He left her with so many unanswered questions. Her life was a mess.

- **Guilt**. Many who grieve feel remorse or regret that they either did or did not do something for the departed. A daughter told me that the decision to take her mother off the hospital life-support system made her experience extreme guilt.

- **Abandonment**. This is the sense that we have been left behind after the death of our loved one. One widow told me that she missed her husband of 54 years—so much that she wanted to die so she could join him.

- **Loneliness**. A feeling that we are slipping into isolation can cause great pain. A mourner told me, "Sometimes I feel I am all alone with no one to turn to, especially when important decisions have to be made."

- **Fatigue**. Grief work can be exhausting and fatigue is part of the process. "I have no energy. I am always tired." These are common responses from people who mourn.

- **Shock**. If the death is sudden or unexpected—or if the mourner is somehow not prepared for the death— then shock might be a part of the grief process.

- **Helplessness**. Many people feel vulnerable and defenseless during grief. With tears and a trembling body, a woman told me that her deceased husband had done everything for her and she now felt utterly helpless.

- **Freedom or Emancipation**. This is often a positive feeling experienced by those who felt controlled or restrained by the deceased. I recall hearing from an adult child of an alcoholic who had been the caregiver for her abusive father. After his death, she felt relieved to be liberated from his tyranny. Others can have this feeling of release when their loved one suffered a lengthy or particularly painful illness. Why am I listing this among possible sources of grief pain? Sometimes, feelings of freedom after a death can circle back and fuel our feelings of guilt and hurt.

As we feel the pain of grief, we may be going through some or all of the above experiences. Determining how long a person's grief will hurt is often related to a mourner's willingness to address these underlying sources of pain. There are many ways to address these issues, among them: attend grief ministry workshops; counsel with clergy; talk with mature friends; see appropriate professionals; and stay spiritually, mentally and socially active.

Do not be alarmed if some of the following behaviors occur. Some of these behaviors are predictable and frequently associated with normal grief.

Grief Behaviors

- **Sleep Disorders**. Sometimes mourners experience difficulty going to sleep or they awaken very early. Others want to sleep all the time and allow sleep to become a means to forget their pain. A widow told me she tried to stay awake and active as long as she could every day because the bed was so lonely.

- **Appetite Disorders**. Overeating and under eating are frequent grief behaviors. Changes in weight are often experienced in the grief process. People who are mourning often say things like: "Nothing tastes good to me. Much of the food I eat reminds me of her and it hurts."

- **Absent-minded Behavior**. It is not unusual for the bereaved to become forgetful, neglectful and confused during grief. One mourner told me he could not remember names, addresses or phone numbers that were common to him before his loved one died.

- **Dreams of the Deceased**. It is quite normal to dream of the dead. Sometimes these dreams are positive and pleasant while at other times the dreams can feel like nightmares. One night after my father died, I dreamed that he was talking to me and telling me that a certain situation would be okay and that he was proud of me.
- **Restless Over-activity**. Many people use hyperactivity as an escape from facing their grief.
- **Crying**. Tears during grief are widespread for both men and women. Tears can be therapeutic, according to medical studies. Of course uncontrollable, continuous crying would not be healthy.

How long will my grief hurt? The sting of grief and its duration are frequently related to the issue of guilt and forgiveness. Here is how one woman described that process after her husband died:

"After suffering with Alzheimer's for seven years, my husband died. We had been married for 53 years. As he lost more and more of his dignity and ability to care for any part of himself, I began to pray that God would be merciful. Even then I was ashamed of those prayers and now I do not know what to do with my guilt. How do I tell the dead 'forgive me'?"

Guilt and forgiveness are powerful emotions in grief. Sometime mourners want forgiveness from the dead. There are many healthy ways to pursue forgiveness and relief from guilt. Several steps might be helpful in this process:

- Speaking to a minister or counselor.
- Sharing your feelings with a family member or trusted friend who knows the situation.
- Writing a letter to the deceased and expressing your feelings.

- Allowing yourself to view the situation from a perspective that is outside the orb of grief.

We often want to experience forgiveness with surviving family members. Families live with enormous pressure as they struggle through the end of a loved one's life, then a death and all of the responsibilities immediately after death. Our grief can be magnified and lengthened if there is family tension following the death of a loved one. It is important for family members to communicate their feelings openly with each other and work at resolving differences. Family communication is extremely critical in traumatic deaths, such as when parents face the loss of a child. Divorce is often the unfortunate conclusion to unresolved guilt in this complex process of grief. (See Chapter 9 for more on this.)

How long will my grief hurt? The pain of grief has no easy cure or quick fix. Allow your pain to tell you where it hurts and then focus your energy on addressing that hurt with all the resources you can assemble.

Closing Prayer

Dear God of Time:
The pain of grief has bound me for too long.
I am sad. I cry.
My body hurts all over.
Will this plague of grief ever go away?
Will I ever find release?
How long will my soul be in pain, having sorrow in
my heart every day?
How long, O Lord? How long?
Your time is not my time, O God.
The clock within my soul weeps for relief.
I have lost the vision of Your timeless seasons.
I dream of Your time of healing,
I long for Your seasons to turn:

For a time to build up again,
For a time to laugh,
For a time to dance,
For a time of peace.
Show me Your larger vision of time, again.
And, for today, help me to grieve just long enough
to set my memories free.
In Jesus name we pray.
Amen

Walking Toward Tomorrow

CHAPTER 7

How Do We Deal with Loneliness, Abandonment and Fear?

GRIEF HURTS BECAUSE WE realize that this person we love is—gone. We have lost them in this life, where attachment and loss are as natural as the turning of the seasons. As Ecclesiastes reminded us in the last chapter, life's seasons involve forming attachments to persons, places, things and events—then we are challenged to let go, leave behind and move on. From our first to our last breath, life is marked by loss. But this is extremely difficult to accept after the death of a loved one. Many people who mourn wind up trying to reattach to what has been lost. Grief can either facilitate the appropriate transition from a loss to new attachments—or grief can hinder that transition and create additional anxiety.

Erich Fromm wisely taught: "To spare oneself from grief at all costs can be achieved only at the price of total detachment, which excludes the ability to experience happiness."

Attachment and loss are natural cycles in life. But how do we keep going when the loss is as profound as the death of a loved one? Our faith teaches that God somehow provides for this natural process with a far grander vision of life's ultimate relationships. In Romans 8, we read:

> For I am persuaded that neither death, nor life, nor angels, nor principalities, nor powers, nor things present, nor things to come, nor height, nor depth, nor any thing in creation, will be able to separate us from the love of God, which is in Christ Jesus our Lord.

This is not easy to envision when attachments are broken in death—and we begin to feel our own brokenness as well. As the coffin is lowered into the grave, we feel part of ourselves being buried. Just as attachment is a major part of human life, so is its opposite: abandonment. In grief there is a sensation of isolation and loneliness. This feeling of forsakenness in grief can be evident in many areas of life:

- Physical loss of the deceased.
- Spiritual estrangement from God.
- Social distancing from that which was familiar (friend, church, clubs, etc.).
- Psychological disconnection that allows grief/abandonment to control our emotions.

Abandonment and loneliness produce anxiety that fuels our fears. This can become a serious call for help. The Rev. Paul E. Irion taught and wrote for decades about the many forms of pastoral help we can provide with end-of-life decisions, death and mourning. Irion identified three forms of fear in grief:

1. Fear of death itself. The reality of the death of someone very close to us is an event that tends to personalize death and activate fear of our own death.
2. Fear of the dead person. Our deceased loved one has changed and we do not fully understand what has happened.
3. Fear connected to our own suffering and loneliness. The death of a significant person, in whose life we are closely related, prompts our fear of forsakenness and abandonment.

Our fear in grief is directly related to how dependent we were on the deceased. This may have nothing to do with the amount of love, respect or devotion we had for the person. "Attachment Theory", introduced by John Bowlby, describes this correlation between one's level of attachment to the deceased and the intensity of one's grief response. Knowing a little about this principle can help a mourner move through this painful and disorienting experience. One extremely independent widow told me, somewhat apologetically, that she was detaching from her husband even before his death:

> I watched David slowly die for three years. His disease was relentless. I loved him and I cared for him without regret. Now, I miss him. Yet, somehow, now that he is gone, I have no need for tears.

Because she had anticipated grief, the reality of her actual grief was less intense. Some of her best friends were a bit disturbed at her rather controlled emotions during the grief process. They talked about her lack of tears and whether or not she truly was grieving. They mistakenly were equating her tears and emotion with the level and intensity of her grief. They were not taking into consideration what Attachment Theory teaches us about the process. This widow had started detaching—preparing for this loss—during the long, painful process of her husband's relentless decline.

Bible scholar Walter Brueggemann recommends that we read the Bible's Psalms of lament as a powerful way to help mourners shape their grief. I have often used Psalms of lament with grieving families. From years of working with Psalms in this way, I recommend 50 of the 150 in our Bible:

> To experience the consoling power of these ancient hymns of lament, consider reading Psalms 3, 5-6, 13, 17-18, 22-23, 25, 27-28, 30-31, 35, 38-43, 46, 51, 54-57, 59, 61, 64, 69-71, 74, 77, 86, 88-89, 102, 109, 116, 119-121, 124, 130, 137, 140-143. These ancient lines are dialogues with God. They help us shape our own boundaries and passageways through our grief.

I asked several church members to read lament Psalms and share their thoughts about how these Psalms relate to their feelings of loneliness, abandonment and fear:

> Ellen said the Psalms were voicing her own experience: "I couldn't eat or sleep. I felt my body was going to explode with grief. I felt alone."
>
> Ann wrote lines in her journal similar to what we find in these Psalms: "Sometimes I feel I am all alone with no one to turn to, especially when important decisions have to be made."
>
> Lucy said: "I knew few people whose child had died, and I knew no one whose child had committed suicide. I felt that I did not fit in anywhere. I was abandoned from a social standpoint but not from God." She explained, "Psalm 102 describes perfectly my first feelings of grief—the aloneness, the despair and the physical manifestations." Psalm 102 is the only Psalm of lament that is so described in its title: "A prayer of an afflicted man when he is faint and pours out his lament before

the Lord." (See the closing prayer in this chapter for more on Psalm 102.)

In their grief, people can feel intensely alone. They yearn for their deceased loved one and often they are by themselves for the first time in many years. Adjusting to this new and lonely environment can be difficult. Near the beginning of *A Grief Observed*, C. S. Lewis admits his own anguish after the loss of his wife: "My heart and body are crying out: come back, come back."

Psalm 23 is considered one of the most comforting and popular passages of scripture. Two people in one of my grief workshops had an interesting response to this Psalm. We were discussing the line: "I will fear no evil, for Thou art with me." Sue said that verse bothered her because she was feeling fear and she wondered if this indicated a lack of faith. "I do not like staying by myself and living by myself," she said. "Going into the house at night is a bad feeling." Sue's husband and her mother both died within a few months of each other. All three had lived in the same house for many years. Psalm 23 suggested to Sue that she should not be feeling such fear and isolation. Discussing the passage allowed us to bring one of Sue's central concerns out into the open. Another workshop participant, Mary, also spoke of her fear as if grief had established a total environment of anxiety. Mary told us:

> I was afraid to go into the house. I was afraid to not go in the house. I did not want to go into the bedroom. I was afraid of business, my attorney, my accountant—every time they called I was afraid. I was afraid of everything. I felt that something was wrong with me. A friend says that I have not accepted my husband's death.

Sue and Mary are not alone. C.S. Lewis wrote about his own surprise that grief could feel so much like fear—"the same fluttering in the stomach, the same restlessness, the yawning." And, Mary's realization that fear can come from many directions also is understandable. David K. Switzer, who taught pastoral care at the Perkins School of Theology, writes that fear in grief is conditioned by pain. A person anticipates the pain associated with grief and that arouses the perception of fear. This cycle can churn with ever-increasing intensity.

For solace, many people turn to the church. They understand that grief is related to community and that congregations can be a support for those who grieve. People may reach out to a minister or to other members who have lost loved ones, but grieving people may reach out in many directions. They may seek solace from people in a small group, such as their Sunday school class, a choir, a women's group or a men's group. Some congregations have special support groups dedicated to helping people through grief. Regular worship is often a comfort. The church should be a place that openly feels the pain of the bereaved and embraces that hurt.

For some, however, the church does not measure up to their expectation of support during grief. Meredith and her husband Brad had been members of the church for 35 years. Cancer incapacitated Brad for several years. Meredith had been his constant caregiver. When Brad died, this is what Meredith said about the church:

> I'm in my eighth month after Brad's death and things ought to be getting better. My brain, my intellect, tells me things should be getting better. I know he is not coming back. Some days I so wish he would! Not with the cancer, of course. When he died, I became reclusive—so much so that my doctor had to get strong with me about getting back with friends. I did not even want to be with my friends. I quit coming to Sunday school and church. I dropped out of the choir and the mission group. I sat at home and cried; I cried all the time. My heart told me to go back to church but my body would not move. I could not and would

not get up, put on makeup, get dressed and drive myself to church. It was all too painful, it hurt so bad.

Ideally, the church should be a place for healing, but depending on the circumstances, sometimes the church is not the place where healing begins. Some people feel estranged from the church during grief. For many, grief can be an opportunity to reach out to others—co-workers, family members and neighbors. Often, grieving people reach out to others who have experienced grief. Barbara was 50 when her daughter died in a tragic car wreck. Five years later her mother died after a long illness. When Barbara was 65, her husband died of heart problems that had confined him to their home for two years. During the time she was her husband's caregiver, Barbara limited her activity at church and the community. Six months after his death, Barbara resumed teaching violin lessons in her home. She returned to the sanctuary choir and her Bible class. Within the city, she attended a local grief support group and later volunteered to be a group leader. In her journey through grief, Barbara reached out in many directions—reconnecting with students, a local support group and neighbors in her community—as well as the church. Grief should not be a private emotion. We need to welcome people who have experienced loss in a compassionate way wherever they first make their connections.

How we cope with loneliness, abandonment and fear will profoundly affect the grief process. Grief often creates a protective cocoon that on one hand shields the mourner from outward obtrusive pain, but on the other hand can exacerbate feelings of isolation. Good grief work reaches through that orb of selfish lament so that eventually—often surprised by joy—we may discover that life is not over in the land of grief. God clasps our trembling hands and leads us into tomorrow.

Closing Prayer

Dear Ever Present God, with the Psalms I pray:
Do not hide Your face from me in this day when I am in trouble;
Hear my prayer and answer quickly.
My life is going up in smoke;
my bones are burning within me.
My heart aches; I forget to eat.
In my weeping, tears fall and mingle in my cup.
But, You have been our dwelling place in all generations.
Before the mountains were brought forth,
or You formed this world,
from everlasting to everlasting, You are God.
So, teach me to number my days, that I may apply my heart to wisdom.
Lead me this day beside still waters,
Make me lie down in green pastures,
Restore my soul.
With Your rod and staff—comfort me
I will reach Your table once again.
Surely goodness and mercy will follow me
and I will dwell in the house of the Lord forever.
In the name of the One who is our Shepherd we pray.
Amen
—based on Psalms 102, 90, 23

Comforting Hands of God

CHAPTER 8

How Do Special Circumstances Affect Grief?

GRIEF IS DIFFICULT AFTER any death but when the death is sudden, tragic or the illness is prolonged, the grief is often more intense. Sudden and tragic death can be very complicated for the survivors because there is usually no warning that death is imminent and there are major issues to confront without preparation. In this chapter, I am grateful to J. William Worden for his insight into sudden death. You will find Worden and other helpful authors listed in the Recommended Reading section at the end of this book.

Sudden Death

If the death of our loved one is expected, we have an opportunity to prepare. This process is known as "anticipatory grief." Often, but not always, this anticipation helps to ease our post-death bereavement. In contrast, sudden death is a full-force blow without warning. In addition to the shock, a host of issues caused by this death may seem to explode in your family life. Consider this case:

> Bob seemed healthy and strong but had a fatal heart attack at 67 years of age. The coroner concluded that Bob died instantly in his sleep. One friend said to the family, "What a way to go. You go to sleep on earth and wake up in heaven." That statement may seem comforting, but those words were like acid to Bob's family. With no preparation, no warning—their pain was extremely intense.

Scripture teaches that death, by its very nature, can be sudden. Jesus talked about this in the parable of the rich man who thought he could fill enough barns to enjoy a long life. Instead, in Jesus' story, the man dies suddenly. (Read Luke 12 for the full story.) The Bible also tells us that the sudden nature of death is not necessarily a tragedy. In I Corinthians chapter 15, we read:

> Pay attention, I am telling you a mystery: Death is not what you think. We will be changed—it happens in a moment, in the twinkling of an eye, at the last trumpet. … Then what is written will come true: "Death is swallowed up in victory." O death, where is your sting? O grave, where is your victory? … Thanks be to God! He gives us the victory through our Lord Jesus Christ.

Just as Jesus indicates in his parable, this is very difficult for us to accept. Several factors often surface after a sudden death:

- Shock and disbelief: "This can't be true. There must be some mistake."
- Guilt feelings: "If only I had … "
- Blame: "I know somebody is responsible for this."
- Medical and legal authorities: Grief is often prolonged in cases of homicide, suicide and some accidents.

- Helplessness: The survivor can feel out of control, angry, resentful and aggressive.
- Unfinished business: "He had just retired and we had planned a second honeymoon."
- Lack of understanding: Particularly in sudden death, survivors want to know what happened, why it happened, who is to blame and what they should do next.

By its very nature, sudden death throws a person into the grief process with no preparation. Denial is a major concern that must be addressed. As the work of grief begins, the mourner must first accept the reality of the death and start the process of healing.

Now, let's look deeper into sudden and tragic deaths. This is not a complete list, but these next sections may help families who need to know more about specific circumstances.

Suicide

> Mary was 22. On the day she would graduate from college, her parents found her dead in her dorm room in an apparent suicide by hanging. Mary's father, Earl, did not want to accept the fact that his daughter might have taken her own life. His grief was almost unbearable. How does a parent deal with the death of their child, especially if the death is a suicide?

Earl carried the burden of this grief for many years, but recently found a ray of hope and a pathway toward resolution. One of his coworkers, Glen, had a son who was having many run-ins with the law. This errant son was finally arrested, convicted and sent to prison. Glen was a distraught father and did not know where to turn or who could help. In a display of compassion and empathy, Earl called Glen and told him not to give up. Earl had allowed his pain of grief to be transformed and Glen was the beneficiary of this transformation.

There are many grief issues that arise after a suicide. Worden suggests that the following concerns are common:

- Shame: There is a social stigma attached to suicide. One widow said, "I can just imagine what people are saying about me and our marriage."

- Guilt: Many survivors of suicide have the feeling that somehow they are to blame for the death. They may even want to punish themselves. People commonly say: "I should have known. It is all my fault."

- Blame: Often a survivor will blame others in an attempt to affirm control in a situation in which they feel so out of control. "His teacher should have known!" or "Was his doctor blind?"

- Anger: There is a strong perception of anger and rejection following a suicide. "Why, why, why did he do this and leave me in such a mess?" A loved one's suicide can deepen a survivor's low self-esteem.

- Fear: Suicide survivors feel an excessive amount of fear about themselves and about judgments that may come from society, friends and relatives. Survivors may even begin to fear themselves through concern over their own self-destructive impulses. "If Dad killed himself, I wonder if I am next?"

- Distorted thinking: Myths—fabricated "truths"—often are created after a suicide. Because survivors may not want to believe the reality of the death, they fashion a contrived story as an explanation. One mother told me she was sure her son's death was due to a mistake he made with drugs and alcohol and not a deliberate overdose.

Of course, these issues may arise after any type of death. But, after a suicide, these feelings can erupt. Grief is complicated by multiple concerns from legal issues that may arise to whatever complex unfinished business your loved one left behind. Wayne Oates suggests several ways to assist a person grieving from a suicide:

- Gather all the information possible about the death, including documents from police, physicians and coroner.

- Keep in touch with reality—especially through strong contact with church, friends and health professionals. Suicide can seem surreal to the survivors.

- Have a family gathering to talk through questions. Invite professionals to join the discussion, such as: a family physician, psychiatrist or clergy.

Tragic Events

I was praying with my friend Wayne Hunsucker at our usual time and place on that Tuesday, September 11, 2001. The word came that tragedy had struck in New York, Washington, D.C. and Pennsylvania. For a moment, we froze in disbelief. Then, Wayne and I contacted our far-flung family and friends. We confirmed safety for all. That afternoon, I appeared on local television and spoke briefly about corporate grief and answered phone calls from the community. Our church opened its doors for prayer and meditation. We planned a special community service of scripture, prayer and music. Church members gave $30,000 to a relief fund destined to help survivors in New York. Through it all, each time I heard our national pledge or sang a patriotic song, I would cry.

Corporate, communal grief is different from personal grief in that large numbers of individuals are mourning together for a common cause. This can become a galvanizing force that bonds people who would not normally have a common connection. This collective grieving can have a positive impact on the community and also on the individual.

After a tragedy, we often talk about faith. This can be a healthy opportunity to share religious beliefs with neighbors. Rituals and religious traditions are very helpful in such situations. Around the world, for example, we often see that mourners have spontaneously created shrines at the scene of a tragedy. We want to gather and express our faith, our grief and our hope. These occasions help to validate the importance of those lives we have lost and promote healing.

Miscarriage and Stillbirth

Many people tend to minimize the grief related to miscarriage and stillbirth, but the loss felt by the parents is very real and needs to be acknowledged. Parents, especially the mothers, often try to assess blame. Sometimes this becomes self-blame, as if the couple did or did not do something to prevent this from happening. We may need to help parents struggle with their guilt. Parents feeling this loss should not forget other siblings in the grief process. Children, depending on their developmental stage, need to be made aware of the loss.

The couple may have the feeling that their hopes and dreams have been lost. If there are multiple miscarriages, the caring community may not be as sensitive to the ongoing needs of the couple. The church, which should be a community of consolation, can become a painful place because of all the babies and seemingly happy families that fill the congregation. It might be helpful in the parents' grief process to encourage them to consider the following—but all of these suggestions clearly depend upon how far along the child was in development:

- Ask the doctor if you can see the deceased child.
- Request medical details, such as the pathology report, explaining the cause of death.
- Name the child.
- Consider a funeral or memorial service.
- Talk with other couples who have experienced miscarriages or stillbirths.

- Counsel with clergy and/or other professionals.
- Attend a grief support group.

Sudden Infant Death Syndrome

Now I lay me down to sleep.
I pray the Lord my soul to keep.
If I should die before I wake.
I pray the Lord my soul to take.

As I pointed out earlier in this book, this traditional prayer can be horrifying to parents whose infant has died of SIDS or "crib death." The prayer was penned in the 1700s, when epidemics could wipe out large numbers of vulnerable children in a single season. Today, when infant death is thankfully rare, this prayer can prompt survivors to blame God. (I write more extensively about our possible anger against God in Chapter 5.) After a loss due to SIDS, self-blame is common. Here is advice from parents who have experienced this particular tragedy:

> You see yourself as a conscientious parent. The whole responsibility of your baby's life was in your hands—and the infant died. Do not let this heavy feeling do away with your good judgment. Hold fast. Ask your physician for the pathology report. Getting solid information about what happened can be therapeutic. Do not face this burden of grief alone. Find a good support group in your community or congregation.

Homicide

Lucy had no time to process her feelings when her older sister was abducted and murdered. Lucy said:

> When my sister was killed, there were about three weeks when I would get up in the morning and say: This is a nightmare! It's not true! Then I

realized that it was true, and I would sit around in the den and cry all morning. I thought I was losing my mind. I thought I was going crazy.

Even though many people sense a feeling of denial and disbelief during grief, Lucy's reaction was stronger because of the dramatic circumstances surrounding her sister's death. Homicide and other violent deaths can amplify our pain, worsened by issues that are common after these kinds of deaths:

- Police and courts are invasive and the legal process can be very prolonged.
- Often mourners are accused or suspected in the crime.
- Concerns surface with extended family and perhaps with previously unrelated people who may become involved, especially if the news media spread the tragic story far and wide.
- Lack of any anticipatory grief or preparation before this death intensifies the mourning process.

Strong and complicated issues facing survivors of a homicide need to be acknowledged: denial, anger, blame, revenge, guilt and despair. In our grief, helpful responses may include:

- Reaching out to law enforcement officers who can provide both important information and referrals to helpful services.
- Counseling with a trusted attorney.
- Sharing your feelings with clergy and/or other professionals.
- Remembering that this grief process will take more time than most, so be patient with yourself and others.

Prolonged Illness

The illness of a loved one that extends over a long period of time can create unique grief issues both before and after the death. I am writing here about conditions such as AIDS,

Alzheimer's, Cystic Fibrosis, Lou Gehrig's Disease (ALS), Multiple Sclerosis, Muscular Dystrophy and some forms of cancer.

My mother had Alzheimer's for five years before she died. The disease changed her in dramatic ways and it also created multiple layers of grief. Our family was very supportive. We decided to care for her at home, first with professional health care and later with assistance from hospice. My own grief began early as I watched the mother I loved so much become someone I did not know. I took some solace in blaming the disease, as she would say things and do things so out of character with her former personality. But, I felt guilty and would think: There are many things harder to bear than death. Her Alzheimer's raged on and so did my own anger, depression and fatigue. Thank the Lord for my supportive brother, Tommy, his wife Rita, other family members and especially a professional health-care team including hospice.

Mother's death brought some relief. There certainly was relief for her from this mind-bending disease and relief for all her caregivers who fought the good fight and knew that death would bring its freedom. But I can tell you from my own family's experience: anticipatory grief, usually associated with prolonged illness, does not remove the sting of grief and loss, when the death finally comes. Although some might call death "merciful" in this kind of situation, my heart said simply: My mother has died.

Complicated forms of grief associated with sudden death, tragic death and prolonged illness may sometimes be classified as "disenfranchised grief." Dr. Ken Doka, a professor of gerontology who consults with the Hospice Foundation of America, defines this as: "Grief experienced when loss cannot be openly acknowledged, socially sanctioned or publicly shared." There are several reasons for disenfranchised grief:

- Relationships involved are not recognized or acknowledged in the local community. For example, an ex-spouse may have died, the deceased may live far away or the death may be part of a sensationalized tragedy.

- The depth of the loss is not recognized or acknowledged, such as prenatal loss or loss of a spouse after a long terminal illness or the loss of a beloved family pet.
- The person grieving is not recognized or acknowledged as fully a part of the grieving process, including people who are very old, very young or mentally ill.

Whether grief is from sudden death, tragic death or prolonged illness, these mourners need resources for their journey toward restoration. Because of the special natures of these deaths, the journey for survivors may seem overwhelmingly complex—or may take far more time than anyone anticipates. Listen to the men, women and children around us who are passing through these experiences and look for ways to be compassionate, to help them through their essential work of grief.

Closing Prayer

Dear God of Sustaining Life:
What a shock!
Death certainly came in the twinkling of an eye
but not in a glorious way—no, in a terrible way.
What a shock!
I am left overwhelmed.
My peace, my joy, my hope are gone.
I am alone.
I did not expect this. No one expected this.
No one seems to know what to do next.
I confess that I am angry at some people.
I know some people are angry at me.
We are all shocked.

No one seems to understand what I am going through.
Yet, You do understand.
You promise that death is not the victor.
I am mourning, deep in pain,
shouldering a world of woes that have cascaded down upon me.
Yet, I pray—Sustain me in this journey, God.
Few understand the path I am walking now.
Yet, You always have known me.
Travel with me through this darkness.
In the name of the One who promised that mourners would be comforted, I pray.
Amen

All Children of God

CHAPTER 9

What about Those Who Mourn Children and Children Mourning?

IN A PERFECT WORLD, we hope that children would not have to deal with death. Unfortunately in our world, children die every day and millions of children experience grief and loss in a variety of ways. Of course, Jesus himself taught that children should be included in vital ways within our community of faith. In Matthew 19, we read:

> Little children were brought to Jesus so He could put His hands on them and pray for them. And the disciples rebuked those who brought the children.
> But Jesus said, "Let the little children come to me, and do not stop them, for the kingdom of heaven belongs to such as these."

Before you confidently conclude that 2,000 years later we welcome children in healthy ways after a death, consider the story of Nancy. She was a nurse at a hospital where I was invited to conduct a grief workshop for the professional staff. Here is the story Nancy told us:

> My mother died when I was 6 but everyone seemed to ignore me. I was hurting so much that, on the day of her funeral, I finally tried to get some attention. I was loud and obnoxious—to the point that my aunt grabbed me by the arm and in a scolding voice told me: "You must be good!" Then she said: "Your mother wants you to be good and, if you are good, then you will get to see your mother when you go to heaven. But if you are not good … " That's all my aunt said. Her pause told me everything I needed to know! I pushed my grief way down inside of me. Now, I'm 36 and I often relive that day of the funeral with all of the anguish and guilt I felt all those years ago. I'm still angry.

While listening to Nancy's horrific story of grief, I thought about the phrase: Just give your grief some time and it will go away. For Nancy, 30 years was not long enough! After telling her story, she cried. We all tried to console her. She never came back to our workshop sessions.

Children do grieve the loss of a loved one. Some professionals suggest that because young children (pre-school through age 6 or 7) lack certain skills that come with later cognitive development, they do not grieve. Although children do not express their grief in the same ways as adults, there is no question that children do grieve. Let us look at children's grief at various age levels. It should be kept in mind that children, like adults, develop differently from age to age and person to person. The following comments must be understood in the most general of terms.

Pre-School Children and Grief

Young children, 3-5 years of age, see the world in a concrete way. They do not understand the abstract terms that adults commonly use to navigate the world. When a loved one dies, children are often surrounded by an incomprehensible wall of abstract expressions about the death and their family's grief. This difficult situation gets worse, because pre-school children usually cannot verbalize their thoughts and feelings about their grief. They may express themselves through play, art, stories, music and games. Their notions often don't line up with an adult understanding of death. For example, children see death as "reversible." Sleeping Beauty, asleep for 100 years, is awakened by a kiss from the handsome prince. They may assume: Maybe my loved one is just asleep, or perhaps away for a long trip, and will come back. The permanency of death usually is not understood.

Magical thinking is often a part of this age group's response to death. If adults are not open and honest with children, even pre-school children, they will seek their own answers to questions that are often beyond their ability to understand. Parents or responsible adults need to dispel magical and erroneous thinking regarding death and grief—so that the young child can establish new emotional connections with remaining siblings and parents.

When I was 5, my maternal grandfather Papaw died. At the funeral, my first funeral, an older cousin who had lived with my grandparents for several years became extremely distraught. The casket was open in the church. My distressed cousin ran to the casket, put her arms around the dead body and said, "Don't leave me Papaw! Don't leave me!" I thought to myself that death is a thief, taking Papaw away.

Psychologist Rudolf Driekurs, who devoted his life to studying children, taught us that children are keen observers, but often very poor interpreters. They may take in everything around them, but their thought processes often lead to incorrect conclusions. John Claypool, an Episcopal priest who wrote about grief, said that children have two common misunderstandings about death: They perceive death as a destroyer or as a thief.

For me at age 5, death was a thief. If I had maintained that understanding of death, I would have been in real trouble. I would watch three other grandparents die, plus several aunts and uncles, two of my cousins, my father and mother and mother-in-law. As a minister, I have officiated at more than 500 funerals. Thank God I matured in my understanding of death and grief. Most of us do. The point of this chapter is to realize that children do grieve and their assumptions about death may seem bizarre to us, but they are quite real to the children who are hurting. Their behavior may be alarming. Here are some common signs of grief and sadness in children:

- A return to bed wetting.
- Crying for a bottle again.
- Clingy, regressive behavior with parents.
- Self-isolation.

Children Ages 5 through 9 and Grief

As they mature, children begin to realize that death is irreversible. Their loved one is not coming back. The child now begins to question the causality of death: Why did Grandpa die? Children gain capacities for guilt and blame at around this age level. They wonder: Am I responsible? Think carefully about casual remarks we utter, like telling someone: "I wish I was dead!" Such remarks can be confusing and distressing to children who are trying to figure out their role in a death.

J. William Worden suggests that children between the ages of 5 and 7 who experience the death of a parent are a particularly vulnerable group. He says these children have developed cognitively enough to understand that death is permanent but they have little coping capacity to deal with death. Their ego skills and social skills are insufficiently developed to enable them to defend themselves, as demonstrated with young Nancy and her strident aunt. Time becomes a major issue for these grieving children. Often, they are unable to properly grieve in present time and thus they develop a delayed grief reaction. This reaction is sometimes called "inhibited," "suppressed" or "postponed" grief."

The news about children and grief is not entirely bad. Children are resilient. Wide arrays of children's books and even films have been released in recent years that can help children connect with supportive assumptions about life and death. Here is the story of Will, who found a helpful theme in a popular movie and musical:

> Will was 6 when his paternal grandmother died. While sitting between his mother and father at the funeral, he noticed his mother crying. He patted her on the hand and told her, "It's OK mother; it's like the Circle of Life, you know, in *The Lion King*." Will had sufficiently conceptualized death to understand that his grandmother's death was part of a universal plan. He understood that all things die: plants, pets and people. Will saw his parents and himself, as future generations forming that circle of life. A Disney theme had helped Will put this death in perspective.

Children Aged 10 and Older and Grief

As children approach puberty and adolescence, their understanding of death and grief is more highly developed. Their ability to communicate their feelings and concerns gives them the opportunity to approach mourning with more adult-like behaviors. David Balk is a leading expert on bereavement in adolescents. He describes the full scope of adolescence as possibly running from ages 10 to 22 and he sees three crucial tasks that adolescents face in overall development:

1. To determine a direction or focus for work as an adult.
2. To become an autonomous individual.

3. To maintain intimate friendships and relationships.

Adolescents are particularly vulnerable during grief. They are not only dealing with their own maturation but also with practical changes that may face them after a death. The stress of grief can threaten the completion of their development into healthy adulthood. When adults cope with grief, they may grow, their faith may mature and they may find a renewed confidence in dealing with life. The same might be true for adolescents, but grief can also overwhelm them, leaving them emotionally, psychologically, socially and spiritually devastated. Because of this, many of the manifestations of grief that we already have described in this book are intensified at this age. In my own adolescence, I struggled with some of these issues:

When I was 12, one of my favorite cousins was killed in a tractor accident on his family's farm. My grandmother's home became the site of a family wake that lasted three days. I am sure the funeral director did his best but Bobby's young body was extremely malformed due to the severity of the accident. I remember visiting with relatives and friends, enjoying lots of good food and listening to family stories. Then it happened: Grandmother took me by the hand and wanted me to go with her to view Bobby's body. The more I refused, the more she encouraged, telling me, "This is the thing to do." Reluctantly— very reluctantly—I was persuaded to approach the casket. The 12-year-old boy in the box did not look like Bobby. The viewing was less than comforting for me but it seemed to satisfy my grandmother. I learned two things at that moment: Death does change things and I needed to face that reality; and second, sometimes observing a family tradition is important, even if it may be uncomfortable.

I am not suggesting that all children should view the bodies of deceased loved ones. It is important to ask the children about this. When my father died, my children were 10 and 12 years old. They briefly attended the visitation at the funeral home; they sat with my wife and me during the funeral, and accompanied us to the cemetery. At the visitation, they were hesitant about viewing Papa's body. We told them it would be their decision. As the family had a private time with my father, my children sat in a nearby chair and watched as we said our goodbyes. Before the casket was closed, they asked if they, too, could say their goodbyes. My wife and I stood with them as they expressed farewell to Papa.

How to Help Grieving Children

Helping children cope with grief requires a caring adult who is patient and tolerant. Children of all ages come at grief from as many diverse points of view as do adults. Here are a few suggestions to help grieving children:

- Listen to the child. Don't answer questions the child is not asking. Listen carefully to the concerns and questions of the child. Adults often impose their own agendas on children and that is not helpful. Consider framing your communication with the child in these three questions: What does the child want to know? What does the child need to know? What can the child understand?

- Do not try to fix everything. Death, loss and bereavement are realities that require time and work. Be patient with the child and allow them to help set the pace for grief work. Funerals and memorials for the deceased are positive organizing experiences for survivors. When appropriate, children should participate in planning and attending these ceremonies.

- Particularly with young children, allow and encourage them to engage in play, to tell stories, to draw and to use music. Adults could consider reading to the children on themes related to grief.

- For school-age children, help might be needed with their peers. Adults should inform the school and church about the loss and how the deceased was related to the child. Explain to the child about behaviors they might see from other people: crying, fatigue, irritability and confusion. Such explanations can comfort children and permit them to accept their own similar behavior. Talk to the child about dreams. It is quite common for adults and children to dream of the deceased, both pleasant dreams and distressing nightmares.

- Remembering and forgetting are challenges during grief. Adults and children must deal with the complexities of memory. Just after the death, our thoughts of the deceased are extremely intense. Time and appropriate grief work allow us to relocate emotions and memories of the deceased. Sometimes the process of relocation makes adults and children think we are forgetting and disrespecting our loved one. This feeling is natural. Children should be reminded that God gave us a good gift in memory. This could be an appropriate time to look at pictures, show them mementos and tell stories about the deceased. Visiting the gravesite from time to time can also be helpful.

- Professional help might be needed for some adults and children. Most people can work through the grief process with supportive family, friends, and church. Unfortunately, not all children come from high-functioning families with the capacity to help them through these difficult challenges. Dysfunctional family systems can leave children and adults without appropriate structures in which to deal with their grief. This is where church, health-care systems, school systems and professional counselors can help.

Adults Mourning the Loss of a Child

The death of a child is extremely traumatic for the parents and the child's significant others: siblings, grandparents, extended family and friends. (In Chapter 8, you will find more information about certain kinds of deaths involving children.)

When a child dies, questions flood our minds: Why did this happen? What possible meaning is there to the death of a child? How could God allow this to happen? How can we go on without our child? Psychologist Catherine M. Sanders speaks of mourning children in phases. Like Kübler-Ross and Parks and Worden, Sanders sees the bereavement process in overlapping phases. The process is not linear and often a person may move back and forth from phase to phase, or not experience a phase at all. Overall, the phases are likely to be:

- **Shock:** Shock, denial, and numbness create a long and difficult grief process for those who mourn the death of a child. The denial phase can last much longer— sometimes a year or more. This period provides an insulation and protection from the reality of such a tremendous loss. As grief work is allowed to continue, the pain associated with the reality of the death indicates that the bereaved adults are moving toward a second phase.

- **Awareness of Loss:** The full knowledge and acceptance of the loss of a child brings with it emotional disorganization. Grief, in this phase, can be expressed through anger, guilt, blame, shame, frustration and extreme sadness. The parent feels not only that their child has been taken away, but also that their whole world is unsafe and meaningless. Survivor guilt is a natural emotion, but in these cases fundamental role relationships have been upset. Children are supposed to bury their parents and when the opposite occurs life can seem terribly unnatural. If parents feel they have failed in their responsibility of caring for the child, then shame and blame can intensify in the family.

- **Withdrawal:** The emotional energy released so far wears heavily on the bereaved parent. They now must struggle to conserve what little energy is left. They may withdraw into depression. Or, they may move into an intentional rest, which is different than clinical depression. Think of King David's lament at the tragic loss of his son: "Can I bring him back again? I will go to him, but he will not return to me." (Read II Samuel 12 for more of that story.) This phase can take a long time. For some parents, it might go on for years.

- **Healing:** This is a time when the energy stored up is directed toward healing. Parents begin to search for meaning in life beyond the deceased child. They begin to understand the phrase: If you don't let your loved one die, they won't let you live. Parents begin to talk about "letting go"—not that they could ever forget their child—but now they may be able to relocate their dead child into appropriate memories. Now, as they focus on others—maybe other children, their spouse, family and friends—and as they look toward their own future, they begin the important task of healing.

Marital Problems After the Loss of a Child

Professionals predict that the vast majority of couples grieving the death of a child will experience difficulties in their marriage. This is not to say that all grieving parents will divorce but most couples will have some serious misunderstanding during the grief process. Concerns in most marriages arise because grief is a very singular process. These two individuals do not and cannot grieve in the same way, so there usually are misunderstandings that arise between them. Family, friends and the church can form an essential supportive network for the couple as they attempt to interpret differing points of view.

Together, the couple can bring resolution to their grief. It will take time, work and much pain. One source of solace over thousands of years is found in Psalm 23: "Yea though I walk through the valley of the shadow of death, I will fear no evil for thou art with me." God is with us through our grief and will see us to the other side, if we allow the Creator and Sustainer to walk with us, even to the end.

Closing Prayer

Dear Father:
We are all Your children in need of comfort and care.
From the youngest child to the oldest adult,
You are our refuge and strength.
We need You especially in our grief.
For those children who must help to bury the dead,
protect their faith through Your redeeming grace.
Show them that new life continues to sprout around us,
that hope is never extinguished,
and that we can learn much about a good life through our grief and remembrance.
For those adults who must bury their children,
protect their struggling faith and struggling relationships.
Remind us that You always open Your arms for Your children.
As we walk through death's dark valley,
among shadows of fear and insecurity,
embrace our frightened souls and guide us along the way.
As Your children, we pray in the name of Jesus,
who taught that the Kingdom of Heaven belongs to such as these.
Amen

The Light of the World

CHAPTER 10

Is Ultimate Good Possible from This Loss?

"WE KNOW THAT ALL things work together for good for those who love God, for those who are the called according to His purpose."

—*Romans 8:28*

Is it true that all things work together for good? This book opened with troubling questions and, in conclusion, we look at the toughest: Can any good result from this loss and pain? Theologian Leslie D. Weatherhead's book, *The Will of God*, written in the midst of World War II, has guided several generations through confusing questions about death, grief and loss. Penned by Weatherhead in Britain as the whole world was experiencing catastrophic loss, the book proposes a threefold understanding of God's will:

1. The intentional will of God: God's ideal plan for humanity.

2. The circumstantial will of God: God's plan within certain circumstances.
3. The ultimate will of God: God's final realization of His purposes.

In chapter 5, I wrote about Bill and Sue and their grief over a stillborn infant, Baby Jennifer. Sue asked a poignant question, "And how could God do this or allow this to happen?" She was assuming that this death was the intentional will of God. My unspoken response to Sue was: No, God does not intend for babies to die. Of course, this was not what I said to Sue and Bill on that rainy Friday afternoon at that initial meeting in their family room. That was not the time to have a conversation about theology. She was not asking me to explain Weatherhead's threefold will of God. On that occasion, I listened, cried, prayed and comforted a grieving couple. There would be other times to discuss the will of God.

But, let's address the question: Why did Sue's baby die? The answer is: Physical complications ended this life. Was it God's will? As Weatherhead explains it, God is Creator and Sustainer of our world, and that means God set in motion a wondrously complex world where an almost infinite number of cause-and-effect processes unfold around us all the time. Yes, death is part of this life for every one of us, but God is not a murderer, Weatherhead argued passionately. Remember that he was writing his book in an era when millions of people were dying around the world, so his affirmation did not come lightly. All of his readers understood that wars can break out and kill millions, but Weatherhead argued that it is not God's will for people to die this way. We die because of events that unfold in this world. We all die at some point. Even in a time of peace, if we fall from a 10-story building or our car veers off the freeway into a tree, we are likely to die. In Sue's pregnancy, medical problems arose and caused the stillbirth.

Can we say there is some ultimate good in this death? Here is where Weatherhead leads us in his analysis: God is not a murderer, but God can work for good in all circumstances. There is the possibility within every tragedy that God can forge a future of renewed hope. Because of what happened in Sue's pregnancy, her doctors might have learned something that would help prevent another death. After this tragedy, it is possible that Bill and Sue are better parents because of their heightened awareness of life's precious and fragile nature. It is also probable that our church learned more about the important needs of parents of stillborn children due to the loss of Baby Jennifer.

Let me repeat: Like Weatherhead, I do not believe that God causes tragedy so some ultimate good can be realized. But I do believe that, when God's intentional will is altered by factors in this world, God actively works with us in spite of the circumstances. God can take the bereavement we are now experiencing and allow this grief and pain to carry us to renewed faith.

Still not convinced? Ultimately, language cannot adequately express the ways of God. That's the conclusion of Belden C. Lane, a contemporary theologian who writes about the spirituality of sacred spaces. Lane describes a spiritual experience he calls Via Negativa: the way of the negative. People make choices, he writes. They can choose to let their grief and pain push them down or they can choose to work through their grief and pain to hope and new faith. Sometimes, Lane writes, people need to go beyond all of our religious language into empty places where God can reach us afresh in the silence. Early Christians went to the emptiness of the desert to pray. In his book *The Solace of Fierce Places*, Lane writes that Via Negativa can help us discover "God's presence in brokenness, weakness, renunciation and despair." We find this principle at work throughout the Bible. Thousands of years ago, Joseph suffered painful experiences from the pit of brotherly betrayal to the agony of an Egyptian prison. Yet, Joseph says to all of his tormentors: "As you know, you planned evil against me—but God planned it for good." (Look in Genesis 50 for more information.) No, Joseph's troubles were not God's intent, but God used these evil circumstances to accomplish God's ultimate will. Now, think of Jesus' own journey along the Via Dolorosa, the Way of Grief or Suffering, toward the cross. The requiem of Good Friday is transformed into the Hallelujah Chorus of Easter Sunday. If God can do this for His Son, can He not also do this for us?

John Claypool once told me that he does not believe God causes all of the bad things that happen in the world. However, when humans choose to do bad things, God is like an ingenious chess player. No matter what evil moves humanity might make, God always has a counter move. Whenever we think that bad is winning in the world, may our faith remind us: God is the Alpha and the Omega, the Beginning and the End. God through Jesus Christ has overcome evil.

At this point, I must caution against relying exclusively on triumphant thinking. In the face of a loved one's death, people often are pushed too hard and too fast toward affirming truths that they simply are not feeling—and will not feel for a long time. If these 10 chapters have persuaded you of anything, then you realize that grief is deeper, more complex and longer than most people assume. What I am affirming in this final chapter is this: There is a loving, kind, compassionate, all-knowing and all-wise God who sees our grief and pain. Whatever tragedy life has thrown at us, God's ultimate will is never defeated nor is our hope of renewed life and joy.

Throughout this book, I have recommended praying along with Psalms. (See Chapter 7 for more on this.) Have you noticed how Psalms often are most powerful when they are juxtaposed with each other? The lament Psalm 22 is a fitting preface to the most familiar and beloved of them all: Psalm 23. A person in grief can allow Psalm 22 to express abandonment and then be embraced by Psalm 23 as a song of reassurance and hope. When we read in Psalm 23 verse 4 that God is with us, we are reading the promise of Immanuel, which means "God with us." The focus in verse 4 is moving through the valley of the shadow of death. The goal is not simply to reach the other side. While we are moving, something is happening. Along the grief journey, something is unfolding that is both positive and healthy for our life and faith.

We have asked many questions in this book. Let me leave you with one more: Will our faith have children? I am asking whether the living can learn from the dying. Will there be a future in faith for those who grieve? Are those who grieve willing to let God surprise them? Two theologians ask this kind of question. John H. Westerhoff III asks it this way: Will our children have faith? Walter Brueggemann flips the words to ask: Will our faith have children? Brueggemann adds: "Will we be open enough, risking enough, vulnerable enough, that God may give us a future that we do not plan or control or contrive?"

I believe that the answer to these questions depends largely on how we reflect on the universal experience of loss and grief today. If there is an authentic faith that can lead us through grief, we must have time to reflect on the past, to assess the present and to be vulnerable to a future that God alone can shape.

Is it possible for some ultimate good to result from loss? In the end, the answer is in your hands and in the choices you make. The dead do not grieve—we do. We mourn. We feel the loss and the pain. The only way good will ever emerge from death and grief is for the one who is mourning to slowly, painfully but deliberately begin to see life from outside the closed circle of grief. This takes work. It takes time. But good can emerge from grief and, when it does, we of faith will see anew the face of God.

Closing Prayer

Dear God of new beginnings:
I know there is some ray of light straining,
pushing through the dark, dark clouds of grief.
Save me from giving up.
Save me from losing hope.
Somewhere, sometime, somehow re-creation awaits.
O God of tomorrow,
O God of new beginnings, sustain me today
and grant me blessed memories of yesterday.

I miss my loved one so much!
Keep them safe and remind me that
in Your Will and Way, all of Your creation will soon
be one.
Through Jesus Christ,
Savior of the world we pray.
Amen

Recommended Reading

- Balk, David, & Charles Corr. *Adolescent Encounters with Death, Bereavement and Coping.*
- Berger, Joy. *Music of the Soul: Composing Life out of Loss.*
- Bugg, Charles B. *Learning to Dream Again: From Grief to Gratitude.*
- Bowlby, John. *Attachment and Loss.*
- Brueggemann, Walter. *Praying the Psalms: Engaging Scripture and the Life of the Spirit.*
- Brueggemann, Walter, & Steve Frost. *Psalmist's Cry: Scripts for Embracing Lament.*
- Capps, Donald. *Reframing: A New Method in Pastoral Care.*
- Claypool, John. *Mending the Heart.*
- ---. *Tracks of a Fellow Struggler: Living and Growing through Grief.*
- Clemons, Hardy. *Saying Goodbye to Your Grief.*
- Doka, Ken. *Grieving Beyond Gender: Understanding the Ways Men and Women Mourn.* (Revised Edition)

- ---. *Living with Grief: Children, Adolescents and Loss.*
- ---. *Living with Grief When Illness is Prolonged.*
- Fowler, James W. *Stages of Faith: The Psychology of Human Development and the Quest for Meaning.*
- Frankl, Viktor E. *Man's Search for Meaning.*
- Gowan, Donald E. *The Triumph of Faith in Habakkuk.*
- James, John W., & Russell Friedman. *The Grief Recovery Handbook.*
- Lane, Belden C. *The Solace of Fierce Landscapes: Exploring Desert and Mountain Spirituality.*
- Kubler-Ross, Elizabeth. *On Death and Dying.*
- Kushner, Harold S. *When Bad Things Happen to Good People.*
- Lewis, C.S. *A Grief Observed.*
- ---. *The Great Divorce*
- ---. *The Problem of Pain.*
- Marty, Martin E., & Susan Teumer. *A Cry of Absence: Reflection for the Winter of the Heart.*
- Miller, Patrick D. *Interpreting the Psalms.*
- Mitchell, Kenneth R., & Herbert Anderson. *All Our Losses, All Our Griefs: Resources for Pastoral Care.*
- Murchison, Rodger B. *Grief and Faith: A Study of Effect.* (Doctor of Ministry Thesis)
- Nouwen, Henri J.M. *Bread for the Journey: A Daybook of Wisdom and Faith.*
- Oates, Wayne E. *A Practical Handbook for Ministry: From the Writings of Wayne E. Oates.*
- ---. *Your Particular Grief.*
- Parkes, Colin M. *Bereavement: Studies of Grief in Adult Life.*
- Saunders, Catherine M. *Grief of Children and Parents.*
- Switzer, David K. *The Dynamics of Grief.*

- Weatherhead, Leslie D. *The Will of God.*
- Westberg, Granger E. *Good Grief.*
- Westermann, Claus. *The Living Psalms.*
- Westerhoff, III, John H. *Will Our Children Have Faith?*

About the Author

THE REV. DR. RODGER Murchison is Associate Pastor of the First Baptist Church in Augusta, Georgia. For many years, he has specialized in grief counseling, conducting more than 500 funerals throughout his career and leading countless grief workshops. He formally studied the latest research in the connection between grief and faith while earning his doctorate from Princeton Theological Seminary. He has lectured and studied widely on grief ministry both in the U.S. and overseas, including doing research at Oxford University's Regent's Park College.

Colophon

READ THE SPIRIT BOOKS produces its titles using innovative digital systems that serve the emerging wave of readers who want their books delivered in a wide range of formats—from traditional print to digital readers in many shapes and sizes. This book was produced using this entirely digital process that separates the core content of the book from details of final presentation, a process that increases the flexibility and accessibility of the book's text and images. At the same time, our system ensures a well-designed, easy-to-read experience on all reading platforms, built into the digital data file itself.

David Crumm Media has built a unique production workflow employing a number of XML (Extensible Markup Language) technologies. This workflow, allows us to create a single digital "book" data file that can be delivered quickly in all formats from traditionally bound print-on-paper to digital screens.

During production, we use Adobe InDesign®, <Oxygen/>® XML Editor and Microsoft Word® along with custom tools built in-house.

The print edition is set in Minion Pro and Myriad Pro fonts.
Cover art and Design by Rick Nease:www.RickNease.com.
Original illustrations by Sara Pollock Searle.
Editing by David Crumm.
Copy editing and XML styling by Celeste Dykas.
Digital encoding and print layout by John Hile.

If you enjoyed this book, you may also enjoy

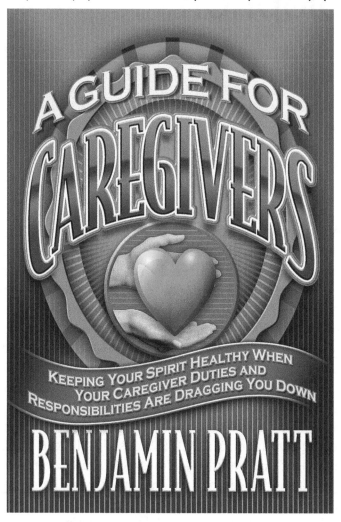

In one out of three households, someone is a caregiver: women and men who give of body, mind and soul to care for the well being of others. They need daily, practical help in reviving their spirits and avoiding burnout.

http://www.GuideForCaregivers.com

ISBN: 978-1-934879-27-6

If you enjoyed this book, you may also enjoy

Dancing My Dream is my story of preserving Native American culture while living in three sometimes conflicting nations: Odawa (or Ottawa) and Lakotah— and as an American citizen as well.

http://www.DancingMyDream.info

ISBN: 978-1-934879-16-0

If you enjoyed this book, you may also enjoy

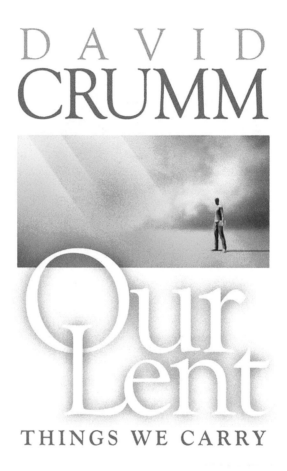

DAVID
CRUMM

Our
Lent

THINGS WE CARRY

"Our Lent" is a 40-chapter journey with Jesus, written by award-winning Religion Writer David Crumm, that pauses each day to explore the enduring power of the things Jesus showed us, many of them quite tangible.

http://www.OurLent.com

ISBN: 978-1934879-016

If you enjoyed this book, you may also enjoy

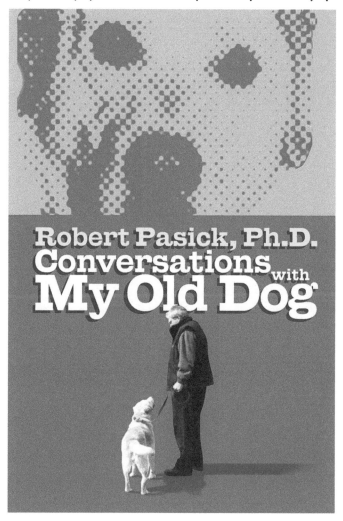

"Subtle doses of humor will bring a smile to your face. Maybe pets really do have solutions to life's perplexities!"

—*An Amazon Reviewer*

http://www.ConversationsWithMyOldDog.com

ISBN: 978-1-934879-17-7

CPSIA information can be obtained
at www.ICGtesting.com
Printed in the USA
FFHW010013141118
49356025-53636FF